I AM EVANGELISM
What can happen when God WINS Your Soul

HASKER HUDGENS, JR.

www.itpublishinghouse.com

Copyright © 2019 by Hasker Hudgens, Jr.

Published by JT Publishing Spartanburg, South Carolina:
www.jtpublishinghouse.com

No part of this publication may be reproduced, stored in a retrieval system, or transmitted in any form or by any means, electronic, mechanical photocopying, recording, scanning, or otherwise, except as permitted under Section 107 or 108 of the1976 United States Copyright Act, without either the prior written permission of the author or authorization through payment of the appropriate per-copy fee to the Copyright Clearance Center, Inc. 222 Rosewood Drive, Danvers, MA 01923, 978-750-8400, fax 978-646-8600, or on the Web at www.copyright.com. Requests to the author for permission should be addressed to the Permissions Department, Hasker Hudgens.

Limit of Liability / Disclaimer: The advice and strategies contained herein may not be suitable for your situation. You should consult with a professional where appropriate. Neither the Publisher nor the Author shall be liable for any loss of profit or any other commercial damages, including but not limited to special, incidental, consequential, or other damages.

Readers should be aware that internet websites offered as citations and/or sources for further information may have changed or disappeared between the time this was written and when it is read.

Scriptures are taken from the Holy Bible, New international version®, NIV®. Copyright© 1973, 1978, 1984, 2011 by Biblica, Inc. TM Used by permission of Zondervan. All rights reserved worldwide. www.zondervan.com. The "NIV" and "New international version" are trademarks registered in the United States Patent and Trademark Office by Biblica, Inc. TM.

Other Scripture references are from the following sources: New King James version®.

Copyright© 1982 by Thomas Nelson. Used by permission. All rights reserved.

JT Publishing House books and products are available through most bookstores. To contact JT Publishing House, visit: www.jtpublishinghouse.com.

Library of Congress Cataloging-in-Publication Data

Hudgens, Hasker. 1965-

I am evangelism: what can happen when god wins your soul / Hasker Hudgens, Jr.

ISBN 978-0-9909925-8-5 (paperback) -- ISBN 978-0-9909925-9-2 (eBook)

2019936677

https://lccn.loc.gov/2019936677

Printed in the United States of America

10 9 8 7 6 5 4 3 2 1

DEDICATION

To my mother, Almena Hudgens, a true evangelist—indeed, you answered the call.

CONTENTS

Acknowledgements   9

Foreword   13

Introduction: The World is Calling   17

Chapter 1: Fishing for Souls   21

Chapter 2: The Saving of a Soul   29

Chapter 3: Purpose Awakened   43

Chapter 4: Becoming Involved   51

Chapter 5: Answering the Call   59

Chapter 6: Wearing Hats, Shifting Gears   65

Chapter 7: Stronger Together   75

Chapter 8: You Are Evangelism	85
Chapter 9: Team Training	91
Chapter 10: Remaining Teachable	103
Chapter 11: Volunteers and Vision	113
Chapter 12: Soul Winning	121
Chapter 13: A Passion for Souls	135
Prayer	139
A Sinner's Prayer	143
From My Wife	145
From My Daughter	149
Endorsements	155
About the Author	159
The Equipping Center	163

ACKNOWLEDGEMENTS

First, I want to acknowledge my father, who continues to live a godly life before me.

Dad, your example of a godly father in the home, reminds me of Joshua 24:15, "but as for me and my house, we will serve the Lord."

As I continue this journey in serving the Lord, I am grateful to honor you and your love for God, your wife (my mother), and your family.

Next, I want to acknowledge my wife. Deanna, I have always prayed to God that He would give me the perfect wife. I prayed for a loving wife with whom I could love, laugh, and do ministry.

He did just that when He gave you to me. Together, the hand of the Lord has been mighty upon us.

You are the perfect wife for me, especially as we serve as Pastors.

ACKNOWLEDGEMENTS

You are a strong companion, powerful woman of God, and so much more. God has truly blessed me in sending you as my wife, and I love you.

I thank God that we get to do life together and impart a love for God and the importance of His kingdom into our children, grandchildren, and great-grandchildren.

To my children: Tamika and Jon, Rashard and Chantha, Christie, Rachelle, Faith, Angel, and Alexander, I love you more than life itself.

I see myself in each one of you. I am blessed to be your Pops. I am grateful to God that we get to serve Him together. I know the best is yet to come! You are filled with greatness!

To my grandchildren, Jaquez, Destiny, Mikiah, Mikel, Zaria, Sydney, Mackenzie, Chance, Nathan, Prince, and Malachi, you are my heart. I thank God for bringing each of you into our lives. I am grateful for the joy and strength I get when I am with you.

Lastly, I acknowledge every person with whom I have served during the sixteen years of leading Operation GO!, one of the greatest outreach ministries in the state of South Carolina. Through the calling of God and His design, we were able to pour out unconditional love and change generations.

Special Thanks

God, I thank You for this opportunity to spread Your Word through this book.

When I accepted You as my Lord and Savior, over thirty

ACKNOWLEDGEMENTS

years ago, the only thing I hoped for was to get into Heaven. Today, I understand. Heaven is available right here on Earth with You.

You are my everything! I could never fully express my love for You in words.

To You be all the glory for all that You give me strength and direction to accomplish. My heart and my hands are gratefully surrendered to You forever.

Jossalyn Wilson and JT Publishing House, thank you for being an instrument in the hand of God to present this book to the world. The assignment was met with enthusiasm, professionalism, and a no-compromise attitude.

Jossalyn, during this journey, you confirmed and affirmed ideas under consideration and brought them to life. As a first-time author, this experience was altogether priceless.

Nytear and Chanda McClain, you are my Dream Team. You two helped with countless hours of editing and laughs. I know, in God, your lives will make a mark that cannot be erased.

To my church family at The Equipping Center, your love and support in continuing the work of the ministry have unlimited value. As we do everything with soul winning in mind, God will continue to anoint us to set an atmosphere where His love and life-changing presence meet every person assembled in worship together.

Your excellence is inspiring. Thank you for five amazing years!

ACKNOWLEDGEMENTS

To God, be the glory as we discover, develop, and deploy our collective purpose in the work of the ministry, and individually, in Him.

FOREWORD

Thirty years ago, God saw a man in desperate need of restoration. A man plagued by drug addiction, fighting a battle that seemed impossible to overcome. It took that man becoming totally vulnerable and open to the power of God for his life to turn around completely. That defining moment put something in motion that caused Pastor Hasker never to look back.

Today, it is my honor and privilege to be a part of his book, *I Am Evangelism*. His book is a true testimony of the vision God placed in his heart many years ago.

This book is a thoughtful composition of the experiences and opportunities God allows us to walk through as we listen, learn, and become the leaders, teachers, and pastors He has purposed.

Through Hasker's testimony, you'll see the evidence of God throughout his life as he has remained faithful to the commitment, he made to God so many years ago; a commitment

FOREWORD

that has been tested, tried and proven over and over again.

The vision imparted in 1988 is as strong today as it was on day one.

What most don't understand, and what you will learn through this book is that walking out the vision God has given you is a rewarding process.

To truly walk out the vision and purpose of our lives, we must do three things:

> *Look up*—seek the Lord in all you do and search the Word of God for direction.
>
> *Look in*—What has God placed in you? I often ask people, "What's in you?" That question forces us to take an internal inventory to find the things God has put inside of us to fulfill His purpose.
>
> *Look out*—take the knowledge of the cross and the love of Christ and apply it to your life and the ministry God has called you to.

This process can be seen through each chapter of *I Am Evangelism* as you read and learn from a strong communicator and passionate leader who knows what it is to receive the redeeming grace of God.

Pastor Hasker has devoted his life to seeking and reaching the lost because he knows what it is to be lost, and in turn, found by a God who loves unconditionally.

As you read this book, I challenge you to pursue the vision God has for your life; don't settle for life as you know it. I

FOREWORD

pray this book leaves you with a new sense of purpose, a renewed passion for ministry, and an urgency to do more than you ever thought possible, with the knowledge of the presence of the Holy Spirit, and the guidance of a God who works in us and through us.

Let the journey begin.

Pastor Bill Wilson

INTRODUCTION

The World is Calling

I will never forget riding in the church van in East Africa after the local host ministry picked us up from the airport.

Our team arrived to spread the life-changing news of the gospel of Jesus Christ throughout the region.

With little to no conversation, the driver laughed, looked at me in the rearview mirror, and said, "So you call yourself an evangelist?" As he continued to laugh, he said, "Tomorrow, we will see!"

Early the next morning, the driver returned for us. He dropped my friend off at a church to preach.

Then, he drove me to what seemed like the middle of nowhere and dropped me off at a huge tent outdoors in a field!

"I'll be back," he said, as he drove away, leaving me with the local ministry pastor.

Little did I know that I would preach, pray, lay hands, prophesy, and win souls to Christ for the next six hours!

God anointed and equipped me to be His hands, His voice, His feet.

Ephesians 2:10 tells us we are God's workmanship, created in Christ Jesus for good works, which God prepared beforehand that we should walk in them.

I did not call myself an evangelist. It is the good work God created for me before I was born.

In fact, "evangelist" does not speak to a title but a specific function. It is not meant to label a person but rather reveals what a person has been anointed by God to do. An evangelist is someone who shares the good news of Jesus Christ with instructions to receive salvation.

My story is about being found, discovering purpose, establishing vision, changing lives, and honoring God as I seek to live life abundantly, win souls, and teach others to do the same.

The Lord taught me to understand the importance of teambuilding and teamwork. As we experienced the benefits of listening, waiting, observing, and obeying the voice of the Lord, we enjoyed success.

The Lord also taught me about evangelism in the trenches, with the help of two powerful men of God, Pastor Bill Wilson, and Pastor Ron Carpenter.

INTRODUCTION

Pastor Bill Wilson of Metro World Child in Brooklyn, New York, is one of the greatest street pastors in the world. He taught me the value of each life, the importance of earning trust, and how to present Jesus irresistibly and responsibly.

Pastor Ron Carpenter of Redemption World Outreach Center, now located in San Jose, California, stretched my vision for the community and supported the birth of one of the most effective, life-changing experiences for thousands of people, including myself, called Operation Greenville Outreach.

Operation Greenville Outreach, affectionately known as Operation GO! or OpGO, was a human bridge that made it possible to make personal connections between the church and the individual in the community, from service to relationship to salvation.

This ministry changed every life it touched.

Over the years, Operation GO! took the Word of God into more than twenty communities in Greenville, South Carolina.

Using what I learned from Pastor Bill and Pastor Ron, I continued to serve God and share the life-changing news about Jesus at home and abroad.

The many lessons learned about street ministry and evangelism are practical, time-proven, and shared in the pages of this book.

As you read, be inspired to look within and answer what I believe is the most relevant questions in personal ministry: *What is God calling me to do to make a difference in my community and in the lives of those I encounter?*

I AM EVANGELISM

Give yourself the space to reflect upon your journey and seek understanding of how God is connecting the dots in your life. Your dots, or experiences in life, helped to define who you are today.

See each principle shared as a door—an opportunity to explore a new concept, or an opening to consider different strategies to strengthen your efforts.

At the end of each chapter, consider the questions, and capture your thoughts and ideas. At the end of this reading, seal your work and your thoughts in prayer.

As you lean in, the most relevant question in personal ministry will present itself again.

Say it loudly to awaken your spirit, "What is God calling me to do to make a difference in my community and in the lives of those I encounter?"

Answer the question with certainty because the world is calling!

Around the city, state, nation, and abroad, people call me the "*Evangelist Guy*," so I guess…**I Am Evangelism!**

CHAPTER 1

Fishing for Souls

"Do not be afraid. From now on you will catch men."
—Luke 5:10

Wearing red t-shirts during the warm months and black hoodies during the cold months, we parked our vehicles along the side of the street, got out, and didn't look back.

Knock! Knock!

"Who's there?"

Standing there, we couldn't wait to meet the person on the other side of the door. We couldn't wait to learn their name, hear their story, learn how we could support their journey, and help steward their relationship with Jesus Christ.

My excitement increased door-by-door as I was able to see the hand of God moving in the lives of people who desperately needed a Savior, just as I did.

With each knock, there was a new opportunity to show our

I AM EVANGELISM

faith, share genuine love, and win a soul for the Kingdom of God.

Street ministry shaped my life and revealed the gains and the difficulties of evangelism.

Evangelism reminds me of fishing. When fishermen go out, there are few guarantees, if any.

Although prepared, the day could become long and seemingly produce little to no results.

However, we wait with expectation.

We continue to bait the hook and swing the rod. As we watch the line go into the water, we anticipate the bite.

Consider the four fishermen in the book of Luke.

It was a seemingly regular day, yet, in an instant, they were called to become disciples—followers of Jesus Christ.

Four men, living their lives, working as fishermen, in their daily routine, were called while washing their nets.

After coming up short on a day's work, the men were likely frustrated, feeling defeated, smelly, and ready to go home.

Enter Jesus, the great encourager.

He looks at them and sees the church, not the building, but the body of people.

He encouraged the men to launch out into the deep and let down their nets for something they had not been able to accomplish all night.

Tired and possibly unsure, they looked at this stranger and agreed to go out one more time.

Their obedience changed their lives forever.

Their nothing became something because God was involved.

Like the fishermen, soon to become disciples, you may be tired of disappointing results produced by your strength and your ideas.

You may be washing your nets willing to return home empty-handed, but what if Jesus asks you to go out further and cast your net one more time?

Sometimes God will ask us to do what seems strange and unconventional in the daily routines of our lives.

Never be afraid to do what God asks of you, especially when others won't do it.

When God Himself makes the request, purpose is present.

You will never go wrong with Him.

Jesus asked the disciples to fish during the day when other fishermen went out at night. This strange request went against their way of thinking and the fishing culture of that time. Somehow, within themselves, they knew to agree.

Similarly, many people are encouraged to engage in evangelistic efforts around predictable times like Thanksgiving or Christmas, but God may need you to fish during strange times when everyone else has washed their nets.

He may need you to go to places where no one else has gone. He may ask you to return to a familiar place where, previously, you caught no fish at all.

He may even delegate you to get out of the shallow water and launch into the deep.

"Holiday Fishing," evangelizing only during the holiday season, will not provide the consistency or relational foundation God needs or desires for real life changes to occur.

Predictable "fishing schedules" like Holiday Fishing with no consistency and no relationship often provide great bait but no catches.

Listen for God. Go deep and leave the results to Jesus!

At His word, the fishermen did what seemed like a waste of time. In one act of agreement, they experienced so much success that the results challenged their equipment and changed their purpose for living.

Their obedience resulted in an exponential, uncontrollable blessing. They had to call for their partners to witness and help manage this life-changing event. The blessing of the Lord was too great for only a few fishermen.

"Evangelistic Fishing" is reaching large and small amounts of people through strategic outreach efforts where you form partnerships to serve a city or community better.

Carefully chosen partners strengthen the ability to haul the nets bursting with fish. Distribution chains are stronger with smart, like-minded partnerships. When you marry God's strategies with available resources, fishing becomes limitless.

After the fishermen pulled in the catch, they were astonished at the results.

When we follow Jesus, He will transform us from great fishermen (soul winners, evangelists, servants) to disciples who get to partner with Him and experience unbelievable outcomes!

With God, nothing shall be impossible for those who believe, agree, and submit to His will and plan.

In the midst of the fisherman's amazement, Jesus confirmed their purpose! They hung up their nets and became disciples, fishers of men.

He said, "From now on, you will catch men" (Luke 5:10).

Although I am sure the fishermen did not fully understand what He meant, they knew to bring their boats to land and never look back.

It was the "Jesus Effect." It is that moment when you know you have encountered the life-changing investment of love from God and nothing in your past matters as much as staying connected to His flow. One encounter with Him changed their life, and they were committed to His every word.

The same is true for us today.

Once we see His goodness, His kindness, and His desire for our success, it is to our advantage that we change our minds and see life through His eyes.

When we agree to follow Jesus, love is birthed inside us, compelling us to share with others through witnessing and evangelizing.

While we have different paths in life, when we share Jesus with others and see the light come on in their eyes, He becomes the difference maker.

Ministry is not a job. It's a way of living.

Ministry is not a burden. It's a joy.

Ministry is not something we have to do. It's a privilege we get to do!

When we identify our place in God's world, we discover what we were born to do.

As the Word of God develops and transforms us, we are deployed by God to reach the people we were born to influence, helping them identify their place as well.

It is a living cycle that sets the captives free, giving life to purpose and direction.

"Fishing" requires patience, but it teaches us to stay the course. It empowers us to venture into different strategies and think beyond our limitations to make the catch.

Develop a patient spirit.

Be willing to invest time and energy. Cultivate relationships.

Build partnerships. Establish trust.

Free yourself to become creative with your efforts.

Think outside the box of what is currently possible and predictable. Genesis 1:1 opens, "In the beginning, God created…"

Being made in His image and likeness, we should create, too.

Be creative! Reach the lost!

I promise every soul is worth it.

I AM EVANGELISM

Questions to Consider

Do you remember the *first time* you went fishing for souls?

When was the *last time* you went fishing for souls?

How often do you witness to those who have no relationship with Jesus or those who are wounded and hurt? What about those who have lost their fire?

What is your greatest joy as a fisherman for Christ?

CHAPTER 2

The Saving of a Soul

"And they overcame him by the blood of the Lamb and by the word of their testimony."
–Revelation 12:11

At age 10, I picked up a basketball and started shooting and dribbling on the community courts.

At first, I couldn't hit the backboard even if someone held me up to the rim.

However, by the time I entered high school, I could dunk the ball during games.

I loved the game of basketball so much it kept me awake at night.

My brother, Albert, and I loved to play. We loved to play so much that we often played in the rain.

It did not matter if it was the hottest day of summer or the

I AM EVANGELISM

coldest day of winter, I was going to play basketball.

I played as long as I could, but soon I could no longer afford the injuries of the game. I endured jammed fingers, sprained ankles, and a broken foot—all for the love of basketball.

However, after high school, I needed to decide between going to college, the military, or getting a job. In my confusion and lack of vision, I chose the job!

Working full-time, I could not sustain my love for the game with the physical injuries. However, retiring my sneakers caused other injuries in other areas of my life, spiritual injuries. 1 Corinthians 15:33 tells us that evil communication corrupts good manners.

Working full-time was great, but I began to spend time with older men on my job whose communication led to negative influences.

They introduced me to drugs and alcohol and taught me how to earn fast money.

Soon, I became good at all of the wrong things. I began to make poor choices.

I drank alcohol until I became drunk. I smoked until I became high.

One day, the guys I hung out with introduced me to a white powder called Cocaine, which was much stronger than alcohol and weed.

The music at that time also was a trigger for drinking and doing drugs.

THE SAVING OF A SOUL

In nightclubs, we danced and jammed to songs like *White Horse* and *Mary Jane*.

I recall thinking *Mary Jane* was a love interest. I later learned that the love interest was not a woman; instead, it was enticing us to initiate a love interest with Marijuana.

I had no idea doing Cocaine was riding the "white horse." It didn't take long before I became addicted to the lifestyle of drugs, partying, women, and fast cars.

Shortly after that, I started dealing drugs to pay for my addictions and habits.

Something that started as a way to pass the time, hang out with my new friends, and knock off the edge from a hard day's work, became my downfall.

I started as a recreational user, became a dealer, and very soon, I was an addict.

Addict was a label I flat out refused! I was in pure denial.

A baller, a hustler, and a lady's man—those were labels I thought I could be proud of, but not an addict.

In my mind, I believed I could quit everything whenever I was ready.

I quickly learned that I could not stop using for more than two weeks.

I only stopped on Sundays because I respected the Lord's Day and often attended church. While stopping my drug use to attend church may sound strange, the home I grew up in

I AM EVANGELISM

had rules.

One rule everyone had to live by was waking up early Sunday morning for church service. Staying home from church was not an option!

Although living on my own, I stayed out most nights. Each morning, it was a race against the sunrise.

However, staying home from church was not an option. It was a part of my fabric as an individual.

I would lie down around 7 a.m. and sleep all day, except Sundays. My eyes would always open at 10 a.m. on Sunday with no regard for the time I went to bed.

Without anyone forcing me, I got up, got dressed, and went to church.

What Satan meant for my destruction; God intended for my construction. The seeds were already planted and watered, and God was increasing His Presence.

My parents, my sister, Velda, and members of the First Christian Fellowship Church were fasting and praying for me to come off the streets and surrender my life to Christ.

Aware of their prayers, I remained foolishly angry with them for praying for me because I felt my life was mine to live the way I chose to live it.

The Bible says sin is fun for a season, and I enjoyed the street life. Blind, I conformed to worldly living with cars, lights, clubs, music, money, dope, and women.

THE SAVING OF A SOUL

However, it became increasingly difficult to enjoy my lifestyle because they were praying for me to leave my life of destruction. All I could think about was God, how I needed to attend church, and how I needed to receive salvation.

The Lord dealt firmly with me to surrender everything to Him. He knew the path I was on and was wooing me with His kindness to avoid certain death.

At times, I carried a gun on my waist.

I had become influential in the eyes of people I communicated with throughout the streets.

My appearance was that of a hustler, a player, and a dealer.

I was hard on the outside, but inside, I was a child in need of God.

I needed rescuing. I needed salvation.

Internally, I was caught between two kingdoms. One kingdom called me to conform to the streets, while the kingdom of God called me to be transformed by love. My eyes were opened, but my heart was conflicted.

Compassion interrupted my hustle. I remember having compassion on a single mom addicted to the drugs I sold her.

I went into her kitchen, looked inside her refrigerator, and searched her cabinets to see if her children had food to eat.

I checked the thermostat to see if the children had heat during the winter.

I AM EVANGELISM

It seemed my stony heart had a soft place.

Conformity and transformation were battling for my life.

Silently, I watched my friends. To me, they seemed heartless.

They would take the food out of the mouths of hungry, innocent children to keep their mother as a customer.

The truth is that darkness is the real dealer. It sells false identities to all who will buy in, both the user and the dealer.

I knew the street life was not for me!

I was caught in a love-hate relationship.

I loved the (false) sense of freedom but hated the trap.

I loved the (false) sense power but hated being controlled. I loved the (pointless) dance but hated being the DJ.

I was troubled all the time—nervous I would become arrested, land in prison, or die.

I had continual thoughts of being murdered, believing I would die and go straight to Hell.

I did not want to die. I also did not want to give up my freedom (as false as it was) or become confined to a cell or dorm with a bunch of men all day and night for the rest of my life.

The life I lived was torment!

A few years later, going to complete a drug deal, I stopped at

THE SAVING OF A SOUL

a pay phone to call the person who paged me.

On the walls of the phone booth, someone had placed a handwritten card with the Sinner's Prayer.

I picked up the card, read it, and put it in my pocket.

I carried that card everywhere I went for the next two months.

Afraid to throw that piece of paper away, I did not want my "luck" to go bad.

I now believe, with everything in me, God led me to that particular phone booth. He knew I would not be able to leave that card in there.

I believe He also wanted me to experience His special love and show me He was and is God and, in this big world, He sees me.

I read the card in private every day for weeks.

Then one night, I was smoking with a friend who mixed something in our bag that did not agree with my body.

My left side went numb. I thought I was dying. I drove myself to the emergency room.

While I waited for the doctor, I reached into my pocket and pulled out the handwritten card boldly displaying the Sinner's Prayer. That night, I did not just read the card as I did previously.

I prayed the prayer.

I AM EVANGELISM

Because I thought I only had a few minutes to live, I asked the nurse for a piece of paper to write a good-bye note to my family.

In the note, I assured my loved ones that all was well. I promised to see them in Heaven, as I had finally accepted Jesus Christ as my Savior. I did not have time for Him to become my Lord, or so I thought.

By the time I finished my note, the doctor had come into the room and gave me three tiny pills to restore my body from the effects of the drugs I had taken earlier.

The doctor scolded me and said that if I kept using illegal drugs, I would die.

He was really upset with me, but it showed me he cared. I wish I knew who he was so that I could thank him.

A few weeks later, after my incident, I heard the voice of God.

I heard Him say I was going to make a public confession of my salvation to everyone. He said I would do what I wanted to do for years and give my life to Him.

The next day I went to church and waited on Pastor Bob Inman, Sr. to give the Call to Salvation.

The day I accepted Jesus Christ into my heart, I do not remember the message preached.

I didn't hear the message at all because I was so anxious about my decision.

THE SAVING OF A SOUL

I was afraid I would not have the strength or courage to honor my commitment to God, like all the times before. I was antsy during the sermon. I went to the restroom.

My heart pounded inside my chest. I broke into a cold sweat.

I put water on my face to calm myself down. I was determined to go through with it this time.

I was determined to invite Jesus Christ into my heart and live for God.

Finally, the moment arrived. Pastor Bob made the Call to Salvation.

I leapt out of my seat like he called my name, ran to the front of the church, and kneeled in total surrender.

I cried like a baby.

I cried so much that it was almost embarrassing.

At the same time, it was the greatest feeling I have ever experienced in my life!

Someone kneeled beside me and prayed, guiding me through the Prayer of Salvation.

November 1, 1987, at 12:30 p.m., I became a new man!

Thank You, Jesus! It felt like hundreds of pounds of failure was taken off my shoulders.

That moment removed all my worries, heartaches, pains, fears, and depression, destroying the yoke of the streets

I AM EVANGELISM

instantly. This was true freedom!

My sins were washed away, forgiven, and forgotten by my Savior.

That day, my soul became saved which, positioned me for Heaven.

I became a citizen of the Kingdom of Heaven!

Tears continued to flow, and I was not ashamed because a miracle had taken place in my life. I felt great. It was awesome that God changed my life in front of the individuals who spent countless hours praying and fasting for me for years—including my parents and my sister.

A prayer I have is to meet the person who left the notecard for me in the phone booth when I leave this world.

The next day, I started telling family members and friends that I accepted Jesus into my heart.

My friends, Rick and Reggie, could only look at me. They were confused by my words.

I'll never forget them looking at me with raised eyebrows saying, "Okay!"

Then, as so many times before, they sped off in their new cars with lots of money and drugs, only this time, it was without me.

Sadly, Rick was murdered only a few months after I answered the call and left the streets.

THE SAVING OF A SOUL

Reggie died years later from a heart attack.

The streets were cold, relentless, and hard on the body.

I prayed earnestly for them and others. They saw the change begin in my life as I continued one day at a time.

Many of my friends from that time either died or landed behind prison bars.

Only a few of us escaped and had our story changed by the never-ending love of God, friends, and family.

Everyone has a story.

The people you are sharing the Gospel of the Kingdom of Heaven with also have a story.

In many ways, they need to hear your story, too.

Understanding and being able to articulate your story will allow you to connect with others.

Remember, we "overcome by the blood of the lamb and the word of our testimony" (Revelation 12:11). Our testimony is the story of God's healing and redeeming power actively working in our lives.

As you evangelize and share the Gospel of the Kingdom of God, think about your deliverance and how God sent His redeeming Word and healed your life and saved you from your destruction (Psalm 107:20).

When you reflect on your story, judgment leaves, and God's peace and love are manifested.

I AM EVANGELISM

Sharing your story lifts Jesus and draws hearts to Him. It helps people to accept and receive Him as He knocks on the door of their hearts.

THE SAVING OF A SOUL

Questions to Consider

Have you accepted Jesus Christ as your Lord and personal Savior?

Are you willing to tell anyone and everyone that Jesus Christ is Lord?

Have you ever thought about your story or testimony?

How is God asking you to use your story or testimony to lead others out of darkness and into a wonderful life with Him?

I AM EVANGELISM

CHAPTER 3

Purpose Awakened

"So they went out and preached that people should repent. And they cast out many demons, and anointed with oil many who were sick, and healed them." –Mark 6:12-13

As a new believer, attending church faithfully was critical.

I felt great about myself. Although my new life was challenging, my new mindset without drugs, heavy drinking, and everything associated with street life gave me great joy.

I genuinely had a born-again experience, and it was great!

The smell of the air, the color of the sky, the sound of birds—it was beautiful to me. I could feel the love of God on a personal level for the first time in my life.

Everything was new!

Being a baby in the things of God, I noticed things I had not given attention to since I was a child.

I AM EVANGELISM

My Pentecostal church fascinated me. Seeing people healed from sicknesses and others delivered from demonic oppression and addictions ignited my fire.

The music intrigued me. The singing was the best in the city, and the band was incredible.

The organ, drums, bass guitar, tambourine, and saxophone all had a new sound. The preaching pierced my heart and soul, prophetically confirming things God shared with me regarding my future.

I was content with all of these things and truly enjoying my time in church. Then, God began to speak to me and interrupted my "enjoyment."

He began to draw my attention to the doors of the church and the empty pews around me. He said to me over and over, each week, "There is more!"

With a new vision for my life, my pastor's evangelistic messages challenged me. I took what I learned, said yes to God's call, and decided to act.

I became a bolder witness for Christ as I developed a heart to win souls.

Noticing

While I noticed the newness of things, I also gave attention to the things that seemed missing in many of the churches I visited.

Most of the people were friendly. They were like one big family. However, something was missing everywhere I went, and I intentionally questioned the missing element.

Then, God revealed it to me!

Everything that I enjoyed and sincerely loved in my new life seemed trapped inside the church itself. It was like a well-kept secret. While most of the people were friendly, they also seemed inwardly focused.

Unfortunately, many of the churches I have visited over the years still fit the same description—inwardly focused.

At that time, God blessed me with a wonderful mentor, Brother Bruton.

He taught me how to study the Bible, and his approach motivated me to read and study independently.

With no revelation or prior understanding of the scriptures, I believed everything I read.

Like an infant drinking milk, I was willing to do whatever I read or thought Jesus would do.

I remember reading Mark 6:56 and seeing how Jesus spent time in the marketplace ministering and healing the sick. God was calling me to witness outside of the church.

I purchased tracts to pass out on weekends to help people learn about Jesus. I started going to the local grocery store on Saturday nights to pass out tracts.

The grocery store was the most anointed place in the city to share the good news about what Jesus Christ had done for me. I considered my corner in the grocery store parking lot an invitation station.

Accepting the call to connect with people outside of the church was less about the church members or the pastor and more about my spiritual growth. God had His hand on me, and I loved it.

The more I read the Bible, the more I understood Jesus' desire to have members of His body share His love outside of the church building and throughout the community.

The Need to Act

Soon God started visiting me in my dreams, taking me back to the communities where I once played as a child. In my dreams, the communities had become dangerous places to live with drugs, gang violence, and drive-by shootings.

Truthfully, I wanted no part of what He showed me. It was dangerous, and I had small children. I felt like Jonah who refused to go to the city of Nineveh. Instead, I refused to go to Jesse Jackson Townhomes (JJT). The parking lots where I passed out tracts was safe. JJT was everything but safe.

One night, just a few hundred yards from JJT, I was carjacked. In a moment, God's call became even more transparent. JJT needed God's love, just as I did. They also needed a preacher that would go. How else could they hear?

That's when I surrendered my will and said yes concerning JJT; even when everything in me said to run.

Saying yes meant dedicating myself to God's agenda. It also meant saying no to things that did not align with His plans.

PURPOSE AWAKENED

Within months, we started a bus ministry, but JJT was our first stop!

To my delight, we picked up twenty-seven children and two adults! Eventually, we needed two buses to transport everyone.

I am so grateful that God knows what is best for us. His amazing grace attracted a great harvest at JJT.

I could not have been happier!

Deciding to Act

After being rescued by God in 1987, I spent the next five years growing in God and attending church three to four days a week.

I witnessed for Christ in grocery stores, on street corners, at work, with my neighbors, friends, and old hanging buddies. I vowed to spend the rest of my life on Earth giving back.

I have done my best to honor that vow. In 1992, I became licensed to preach.

From 1992-1997, God expanded my knowledge as I helped three other churches get started. Whatever it took to connect lives with God, I was committed.

Years ago, when I said "yes," I gladly gave my blood, sweat, and tears to the streets I once played in as a child.

My efforts were relentless. I gave everything I had until there was nothing left.

I AM EVANGELISM

I wanted and needed to reach lost souls. I had a new addiction, and God blessed me with a team of people who loved street ministry as much as I did.

The team and I took little time off. We committed to weekends and holidays. We held ministry activities throughout the week. We hosted sporting events, supported afterschool programs, and conducted teen ministry events.

We dedicated Thursday and Friday evenings to home visits. The team visited every family our outreach efforts touched during the weekend. We visited hundreds of apartments, trailers, and homes in approximately 12-20 neighborhoods weekly.

This effort was based on the keen advice of a mentor who suggested, "When you're not reaching out during the *week*, the church will become *weak*."

Behind every door, there is someone who needs you to say yes to God's call. Someone needs your vision to become renewed. Someone needs you to act.

They may not know they are in need, but they are.

They need your purpose to become awakened so that they can become awakened, too.

Become more intentional today! Lives are hanging in the balance.

PURPOSE AWAKENED

Questions to Consider

Have you been given a vision by God to bring change?

What is God calling you to do that no one else is doing as it relates to reaching the lost?

Do you become frustrated or disheartened by the issues happening in your school, community, or place of work?

Do you feel called to do something about the issues affecting your friends, family, co-workers, and neighbors?

What do you need to get started? What has hindered you?

I AM EVANGELISM

CHAPTER 4

Becoming Involved

"Find a need and fill it! Find a heart and heal it."
–Pastor Tommy Barnett

When I started my Christian journey, I knew very little about God, church, or getting involved.

I had a lot of catching up to do and a lot to learn about ministry and church! The one thing I did know and was very passionate about was sports.

At the time, the church I attended did not have a ton of ministries where I could get involved.

As I searched, I found that most of the positions within the ministry were filled.

I was a baby in Christ and needed to sit for a season to personally grow and learn the word of God. However, while sitting still and allowing the Holy Spirit to work in me, I wanted to put my hands to work. I wanted to get involved! I would often wonder if there was anything for me to do.

I AM EVANGELISM

I had been faithful for six months, attending church at least twice each week.

My father and his friends were deacons in the church.

Occasionally, I helped them chop wood for those in need on Saturday afternoons. I still recall the time and place where compassion sprang up like a fountain in my heart.

My Dad and I delivered wood to a frail, elderly woman who lived in a poor, drug-infested community. I did not know that my Dad had quietly built a personal ministry to keep the elderly warm during the cold months. I began to wonder, "What more could I do?"

In part, not having a lot to do while God rebuilt my life helped me identify where I could be of service. God opened my eyes to the world right in front of me.

In my free time, I started reading the daily newspaper in the mornings. I began to watch the evening news when I arrived home from work.

I discovered that young people were committing crimes at a very high rate, right where I lived!

I discovered that almost 8 out of 10 homes were led by single mothers across inner cities in America.

Drugs and alcohol ruled the streets I once played in as a boy, and HIV was killing young people at exponential rates.

The number of people addicted to substances reached an all-time high.

BECOMING INVOLVED

The media presumed the challenges were due to unemployment, depression, or loss of hope.

However, I learned that many of the drug deals in the community were to make money for legitimate needs.

I could no longer tolerate the pain of watching my city and its people crumble. I started asking myself what I could do to help mitigate the problems where I lived.

Watching the news one evening, I saw the report that a young, African American male killed a police officer in my city.

I felt a responsibility to positively impact the things that were happening to young African American men. I had to start somewhere. After all, it could have been me.

I wondered if I could have reached that spiraling young man.

I wondered if I could have saved the police officer.

Enough was enough!

I drove through the neighborhoods and started recruiting young teenage boys to play basketball with me in an effort to spend time learning their hearts.

Our quasi-basketball team became the beginning of real ministry for me.

My first ministry assignment started at the city gymnasium.

I'll never forget the director of the recreation center, Mr. Johnny Jones. We called him, "Mr. Johnny."

I AM EVANGELISM

He helped me reach the young boys by renting the gym to me for $10.00, for two hours. It was all I could afford at the time, but looking back, it was all I needed.

Because of Mr. Johnny, I was able to get twelve teenage boys off the streets and teach them the principles of honor and respect through my love for the game of basketball.

I became a father figure to the boys, and they became sons to me. I was just 27-years-old.

As time passed, God blessed us with various people willing to sow into this vision. Soon, we had enough money to purchase uniforms, which allowed them to play competitive ball.

I registered the team to play basketball at the YMCA and with the city recreational basketball leagues.

Our team was so skilled that some of the boys could have played on their high school teams.

However, many of them had not committed to excel academically and were not allowed to play on that level.

Beyond grades, many of them did not have the discipline either.

Some of the boys attended school during the day, but by evening, they were on street corners chasing cars to sell dope to buy clothes, shoes, and food.

While I worked with the young men and gave them opportunities to feel great and learn more about themselves, it was also a challenge because I had to earn their respect. They

BECOMING INVOLVED

needed to trust that I could show them a better way to live.

Sometimes, parents would reach out for help. Like the night, I received a call from the mother of a 9-year-old boy who asked me to get her child off the street corner.

The dealers had recruited him to sell for them. Back then, many children were targets because if the police caught them, they would likely let the children go; whereas adults caught selling drugs faced prison time.

God led me to the child, and I took him home with me for a few days. He began to participate in church and learn a better way of life.

Today, he is a wonderful adult living a productive life. He respects life and loves God. To have God choose you to reach a life for Him is one of the most rewarding experiences to be had.

I must say, in this process, there will ultimately be that one that wants to challenge you also.

I recall a time when one of the young men jumped in my face and called me out. He was bigger, stronger, and training to become a professional boxer at the local Phyllis Wheatley Community Center.

Although he had excellent boxing skills, I did not back down from him, nor did I show fear.

By not backing down, I gained his respect.

Years later, the same young man stopped by my house with his wife and child. He assured me he was on the right track.

At that moment, I realized that God had used my life, and likely that moment, to make a difference in the life of that young man.

I was so happy for him. The streets had lost another one!

He was living an honest life with his family.

Encouragement Matters

As pastors and leaders, it is critical that we encourage involvement in activities that will affirm purpose and the ability to make the right choices in life.

Encourage involvement in things happening in the church.

Encourage individuals to serve as mentors in a school, community center, political offices, and financial arenas—anywhere they can contribute. Being inquisitive and getting involved led me to my calling.

There are individuals with great skills serving and waiting for leadership to permit them to start somewhere. Help them find their passion!

When people are involved, it shifts their perspective from themselves to others. It also helps individuals learn where they can be significant.

Exploration is healthy and encouraging people to become engaged in matters beyond themselves will allow them to reach others.

Furthermore, the voice of the believer is a critical need for the advancement of people and the Kingdom of Heaven.

BECOMING INVOLVED

Join boards, volunteer your time and talents, and show up ready, willing, and able!

I am sure there is a seat for you at the table!

I AM EVANGELISM

Questions to Consider

What can you do to help people once they accept Jesus Christ as Lord and Savior?

How can you help to integrate new believers into the Body of Christ?

What has God put inside of you that can help save a life?

What are the needs in your community, and how can you make a positive impact?

You may feel like you are only one, but you are one! How can you make a difference? What can you start? When will you start?

CHAPTER 5

Answering the Call

"But you be watchful in all things, endure afflictions, do the work of an evangelist, fulfill your ministry." –2 Timothy 4:5

Drawn to chubby cheeks and little faces, I believe babies are beautiful. I have always had a love for their cuteness, even as a child myself.

When God spoke to me and told me to work with children, He knew exactly what He was doing in my life. Of course, He did!

However, I disagreed with God's direction at the time because I felt like I should have been starting a ministry.

Like many others, ministry to me meant preaching in a pulpit.

When God spoke to me, I felt I had been a part of almost every ministry in the church.

He had allowed me to become an armor bearer for six years to the pastor who introduced me to ministry. What an invalu-

I AM EVANGELISM

able experience, as it established honor in my heart.

God also allowed me to help develop three very young ministries, and I was in the process of helping a fourth. I just knew the Lord was going to send me out to begin a new ministry for me to lead, not just develop and walk away.

Rather, He said, "Go save my children!"

At the time, most of the children were under the age of 12.

As the numbers increased, we started seeing teenagers attend.

Eventually, young adults connected to the outreach but strangely enough, many of them had never heard of Jesus Christ.

I was blown away! I couldn't believe there were people in America who had never heard of Jesus. It was naive of me, yet still difficult to think He was completely unknown to so many—even He was so near.

As such, I gained a new, healthy addiction. Every day, I lived to introduce Jesus to the city I loved and lead as many people as I could to accept Him as their Savior.

Little did I know; the harvest was already prepared but neglected and overlooked.

Somehow, the people I encountered seemed forgotten. They needed a pastor. Although many attended churches every Sunday, they did not know Jesus.

They were not born again. They were simply church members. Some had been active in ministries for years.

ANSWERING THE CALL

On several occasions, God used me to lead senior citizens to accept His son, Jesus, into their lives.

Many of them were hidden in plain sight.

It is the same today. We must be careful not to assume that elderly people are saved.

Once, I preached a funeral for a community leader. During the Altar Call, a 101-year-old lady accepted Christ! Praise God!

One Sunday, there was a woman who accepted Christ while serving with the Nurse's Aide Ministry. She was 89 years old and had served in the church for many, many years.

One day in the neighborhood, the Outreach team found a man dying in a crack house. He was a military veteran and terribly sick.

With our door-by-door approach, God led us to him at a critical moment.

We were able to get him to the hospital just in time to save his life.

After he was released from the hospital, we stayed in touch. He wanted to attend service, so we sent the church van to his house to pick him up.

Glory to God! He gave his life to Jesus Christ the first Sunday he attended!

He had lost hope for life until he met the Life-giver, Jesus Christ.

I AM EVANGELISM

God restored him so beautifully.

God lifted the sorrow and gave him unspeakable joy.

A knock on the door changed his life, but Love saved him and set him free.

God blessed us to get him an apartment and relocate him away from the drug dealers and users who were taking advantage of his aging, frail body and stealing his paycheck every month. He was taken out of darkness and into the marvelous light!

Then, there was the gentleman who was in the hospital, dying in a coma.

While visiting another patient in the same hospital, someone asked me to pray for the gentleman in the coma.

They recognized me from the community knocking on doors and inviting people to church.

The bus ministry had just started to pick up the children in the community, and we needed drivers.

As God would have it, the man for whom I prayed was a truck driver. When he came out of the coma, he came to church the following Sunday and wanted to get involved.

By answering God's call to reach His children, I encountered more opportunities than I knew was possible.

My heart was content. I wanted people to know God. God wanted to use me to perform great exploits for Him.

ANSWERING THE CALL

When you answer God's call, do not judge or look down on the place where He calls you. Only He knows the outcome.

He sees so much further than we could ever see on our own. Trust His plan and purpose for your life.

It has been said that "big doors swing on small hinges," and this is true with one exception. For these doors to swing, they must be in alignment!

Just like doors, our lives must be in alignment with God in order to be our best selves.

When we are out of alignment, we live compromised lives and accept less than what God has for us. However, when we say yes to Him sincerely, everything changes.

Like Peter, God will use you to add to His church daily those who are being as we agree to stay aligned.

I AM EVANGELISM

Questions to Consider

You are called! Now, what has God placed in your heart?

Have you been called to introduce Christ in the marketplace or through outreach?

Are you in alignment with God's vision? If not, why? If so, what are your next steps?

What can you do today?

CHAPTER 6

Wearing Hats, Shifting Gears

"I have become all things to all men, that I might, by all means, save some." –1 Corinthians 9:22

Throughout life, we find that we often wear many "hats."

I am not speaking of real hats but roles and responsibilities that we fulfill.

The last church I attended, I worked on the executive staff and functioned as an Evangelist.

In addition to the evangelist "hat," I also wore the hat of Associate Pastor.

There are so many lessons to learn while working to reach the lost.

While knowledge can be acquired through sermons and classrooms, volumes of priceless learning will occur from hands-on experience.

I AM EVANGELISM

For example, the ministry of outreach and the ministry of evangelism are not the same.

When I first started witnessing and getting outside the church to reach the lost, the difference was not clear to me.

Years later, it became clear to me that evangelism is intentional and straightforward while outreach is relational and wide reaching.

The duties of an evangelist are many, and some of the key responsibilities include laboring among the harvest and leading the unsaved to Christ (Matthew 9:38).

Evangelists also preach the gospel, with signs and wonders following (Mark 16:17-20).

Working as an Associate Pastor and Evangelist, I spent hours in the community, building relationships, and learning how to provide value to everyone.

God taught me how to train others and create a culture of soul winning throughout the church.

Afforded the opportunity to travel to over 200 churches in America and around the world, I was very intentional about stirring up the gifts in others to reach outside of the four walls of the church to introduce Christ to the unsaved, "unchurched" community.

Somehow, I always found myself working with children and their families to help build the family structure because many homes lacked fathers. The good news was, and still is that God is a father to the fatherless.

Many people wrestle with not having an earthly father.

However, God is always available as our heavenly father.

He can do what no other father can do.

He is my model and the one I seek to please.

I believe all children have a place in their hearts that seeks to please their fathers. This approval is so necessary for the development of a child's esteem.

As I met each week with so many boys and girls that did not know their dads, God made it possible for me to show His love as a father figure and provide the sense of belonging that comes with structure, high expectations, and positive affirmations.

I soon learned that under my pastor and evangelist hats was one of the most powerful hats of all—the daddy hat!

Called Daddy: A Fatherless Generation

Thousands of children began to call me "Daddy." Teens and young adults often called me "Pops." Others proudly called me Pastor.

Of course, my birth children called me Daddy, and I especially loved it when they said, "my Daddy."

Statistics have shown that boys from fatherless homes are almost four times more likely to become absentee fathers than boys from a two-parent household.

They have also shown that girls who grow up without a father

I AM EVANGELISM

have a higher rate of entering motherhood before marriage.

Likewise, in impoverished areas, children from single-parent homes statistically have a higher rate of substance abuse and are twice as likely to commit suicide.

Sadly, they also tend to drop out of school and become incarcerated at much higher rates as well.

Countless studies have shown that children growing up without a father in the home have so many disadvantages.

While these statistics are hard to ignore, I believe it is just as painful for children to grow up without a mother's gentle touch.

Spending time in the community, we recognized that many children struggled with anger and self-esteem issues. They also lacked the confidence that children from a loving home often displayed. Whether one-parent or two-parent, love makes a huge difference in shaping a child.

Working with children in this situation, I found some of them showed a great deal of disrespect for people in authority. I believe this is the fruit of a life, hardened by survival skills needed far too early in their lives.

I watched the behaviors of children in the community and those of my birth children. I did not compare my children to the children I was privileged to serve. Instead, I observed the dynamics of each group.

My children were with me weekly to help in ministry.

Although they were the same age as the children who rode

the bus, I could see the confidence they exuded because they could identify with their father, "Pastor Hasker."

As we spent so much time in the community with the children and their families, many of them witnessed the relationship I had with my children. They saw something they wanted in their hearts. Soon, many of the neighborhood children started to call me "Daddy."

When my children heard other children call me Daddy, they would say, "No! He's my daddy."

I later explained to them what a privilege God had given us to share the love of a father with those that needed it. I asked them if they would mind sharing their Dad on Saturdays. They understood and realized that by sharing their Dad, they were helping, too.

One day, however, my daughter Rachelle called for me as I hugged and shared love with some children near me.

I honestly did not hear her because the children had my full attention. Out of nowhere, I heard Rachelle (a little louder) say, "Pastor Hasker!"

I turned around and saw the face of a little girl who needed her daddy just as much as all of the children in the room who wanted someone to call daddy.

Convicted within myself, I could not believe my child had to call me "pastor" to get my attention.

I determined, from that day forward, I would not go the extra mile to win the world and lose my children.

I AM EVANGELISM

I made sure, with all the hats I wore, that I told my children that I loved them every day.

I made sure I attended school plays, dance recitals, and PTA meetings.

I showed up often to have lunch with them and began to schedule father/son and father/daughter dinner dates.

We went on field trips and to summer camps.

As leaders, we wear many hats, but we cannot neglect our first responsibilities.

Sadly, many marriages and families experience some form of separation or divorce, as the result of not balancing ministry well.

Pastors sometimes tend to place the church as a priority before their families.

Deacons pursue the needs of the pastor and members before their spouse and children.

Members neglect time with their family to seek prayer, worship, and ministry.

Children then may grow up resenting church and God for taking their parents away from them when they were young. The truth is that God never took their parents away for ministry. The parents did not have their priority in order.

It is a trick of the devil whose job is to steal, kill, and destroy. I don't believe God would have families destroyed in the name of serving Him!

WEARING HATS, SHIFTING GEARS

With all of the hats one can wear, it is crucial to remain active in our homes, especially with our spouses and children.

Make it a point to date your spouse and be present for your children.

Learn to go into their world and learn about their interests. When you go into their world, they are happy to support you and go into your world.

Introducing Christ to a hopeless, dying world is my world but not at the price of my wife and children. Stay mindful that you don't gain the world but lose your own.

I am so pleased that God granted me the grace to love and support my children while also being present for so many other precious children.

During our time in weekly outreach, thousands of children came to know Jesus by the love and touch of a father figure and people who loved them consistently.

Years later, I was honored with an award called the "Father of City Transformation" given by local pastors where I live because of the privilege God gave me to share pure love with children in the community and lead them to a life with Jesus Christ.

It may seem overwhelming. However, while wearing different "hats," it is possible to lead effectively and serve well. We must purely and wholeheartedly rely on God to streamline our priorities and instruct us which hat is needed and when.

It is not about balance. It's about order.

I AM EVANGELISM

God.

Family.

Ministry/work.

WEARING HATS, SHIFTING GEARS

Questions to Consider

What is the current order of your life? Would those closest to you agree?

With whom is God calling you to share His love as a loving parent?

What are some of the causes you want to give yourself to in the next 12 months?

How will you get started?

I AM EVANGELISM

CHAPTER 7
Stronger Together

"Alone we can do so little, together, we can do so much."
–Helen Keller

My first Christmas with the children in the community was interesting.

A week before Christmas, I asked our bus of 75 children, ages 3-16, "What are you guys getting for Christmas?"

It was almost as if I had spoken a foreign language that no one could understand.

They looked at me, puzzled by my question.

At that moment, I realized they were not getting anything for Christmas.

I think I cried more that year than any other time in my life. A child living in poverty tears me apart.

I AM EVANGELISM

To completely flip the situation, Operation GO! decided to act.

I did not have a warehouse full of toys, nor did I have a bank account or budget with lots of money, but I knew I had to do something.

I called a few people in the church for help. We were able to purchase each child a Yo-Yo for Christmas.

Based on the looks on their faces, you would have thought we gave each one a big bag of gifts.

I can still see the smiles on their faces. The next year, we planned for Christmas!

In November, we purchased a Christmas tree and placed the names of each child on the tree. Then, we encouraged members to choose a name and purchase a gift valued at around $10.00.

Some of the members went all out and bought gifts valued as much as $500.00 or more.

Other members privately adopted families of six or eight people.

I think it meant as much to the members of the church to buy gifts as it did for the families receiving the gifts.

The numbers grew yearly, and I started to enjoy Christmas more than any other time of the year. I loved seeing the joy and smiles the gifts put on the faces of each child because many of them had very few reasons to smile.

STRONGER TOGETHER

Many of the children came from brokenness and misfortune.

We found that one of the biggest challenges for these young, beautiful lives was consistency. From work demands on single-parent homes, aging grandparents, and the busy lives of many other relatives, there were many opportunities for children to be left alone.

We even went to homes where children were cared for by a big brother or sister, who just happened to be 10 or 11 years old themselves. Survival was their daily mission.

There were children dropped off by foster care homes and picked up after service to attend Super Saturday activities!

At this point, the Bus Ministry had grown and averaged 200 to 400 children weekly.

Like most church memberships today, the majority of the children attended two weekends out of the month.

There were nearly 800 people on the roster, but we were only certain about our numbers on Super Saturdays.

Super Saturday was our most significant weekly outreach opportunity. It included working with children ages three to eighteen.

By the fourth and fifth year, we were serving more than 2,500 children, and God was still providing.

As time continued, the Lord added more partners to join us in our efforts. When we are doing God's work, He will send the necessary resources.

I AM EVANGELISM

One year, I got a call from a local restaurant owner, Keith. He owned a couple of restaurants, and he wanted to meet with me.

When we got together, with tears in his eyes, he said, "I want to help. I need to give back!"

He challenged me to go out and find as many people as I could for him to feed. Along with the toy giveaway, he wanted to provide steak dinners to all the families, as he owned two steakhouses in Greenville, South Carolina with the best steak and seafood within hundreds of miles.

We bused families, the homeless, invited foster homes, and men and women's shelters to the annual toy giveaway called Holiday Hope.

Some of the adults there had never eaten steak before in their lives.

Sadly, some put the steak in their pockets to eat later.

The evening was beautiful! We had a great dinner with live praise and worship and the Word of God. We prayed with many beautiful people and enjoyed loving and hugging God's children.

Although we distributed many gifts, we never lost sight of THE GIFT! Hundreds accepted Jesus Christ as their Lord and Savior! I was gratefully overwhelmed.

Then, in March 2003, President Bush informed the nation that he had ordered troops to Iraq. America had close to 192,000 troops in Iraq.

STRONGER TOGETHER

Although it was a nightmare for the nation, impoverished children living in inner-city Greenville would not be forgotten.

In 2000, God blessed us to give yo-yos to 75 children. In 2001, He blessed us to give toys to approximately 400 children. By 2002, 800 children received toys by God's goodness. As the numbers rose, we knew that only God could keep up with the expected growth for the upcoming years.

God had established us as a church where families could receive help throughout the year and especially at Christmas for the hopes and dreams of their children.

The entire city depended on our services. The mayor, police departments, and local communities were involved in God's plan.

That year, we received a call from the Marine Corps Reserve.

They wanted to meet with us. Nervously, we drove to the military base, unsure of the meeting agenda.

When we arrived, the gentleman said, "We are going to war, and we need your help."

Feeling nervous because I wasn't thinking about joining the armed forces, I looked confused.

He said, "We've been watching you guys, and we believe your church can help us because you have a large group of volunteers."

The gentleman explained a program they called Toys for Tots. He shared their strategy and how they placed large boxes inside businesses around the city to collect toys for children in need.

However, he shared their struggle to distribute the thousands of toys they collected because they did not have adequate human resources now that soldiers were fighting in Iraq.

"Will you help us?" He asked.

After praying for about two seconds, I answered, "Yes!"

Toys for Tots and the growing toy giveaway were the perfect marriage. God had answered our concerns regarding the increasing need.

That year, we were reaching thousands of children.

We had a warehouse to store the toys along with volunteers to help interview parents to filter out any abuse. Retirees and high school students bagged toys day and night to distribute the week before Christmas.

The toy giveaway had become so big it outgrew the church's outreach facility and parking lot. The local convention center called and wanted to collaborate with us. They offered a facility that could accommodate 10,000 people.

For the next seven years in December, we packed out the convention center, giving toys to nearly 5,000-7,000 children annually, along with hot meals, clothes, jobs, and, of course, the love of God and Call to Salvation.

Before distributing toys, I preached, and I witnessed hundreds of individuals give their hearts to Jesus. It was a beautiful experience.

STRONGER TOGETHER

What started with 75 children not receiving a gift for Christmas, over time became an event the entire city supported.

One of the men I learned a great deal from over the years is Tommy Barnett of the Phoenix Dream Center (now Dream City Church). He teaches that when we do the uncommon, God does the extraordinary.

It has been my experience that we are often being watched. There are many people and organizations actively looking for partners.

We had great success partnering with the Marine Corps Reserve at Christmas. During the Spring, we held another city-wide event where we partnered with a local radio station called JAMZ.

Together, we hosted a huge outreach several years called City Fest. Our theme for the outreach was "Eggs Equal Souls." To our surprise, ten thousand people showed up for an egg hunt!

While I do not place my faith in a bunny or colorful eggs, I do believe in the Resurrection of Jesus Christ. There are moments when you have to reach the people where they are and point them to where they can be.

We put 250,000 candy-filled eggs on the football field. Before blowing the whistle to start, I preached the Gospel to 10,000 people that generally would never enter a church building on a Sunday morning.

Hundreds of those individuals accepted Jesus Christ as their Lord and Savior!

I AM EVANGELISM

The same was true with the Christmas Toy Drive! Before one toy would be given out, we preached to thousands of people, many without a church home.

All of the hard work, prayers, strategic planning, and raising support was for one reason—to win souls.

Our goal should always be to invite Heaven to earth and introduce people to the King of Kings. His name is Jesus.

When thinking about evangelism on a large scale, we can trust God's word. If we are "faithful over a few things, He will make us ruler over many things" (Matthew 25:21).

We did not always have money to bring to the table, as it related to our role in partnerships.

However, we had connections with the city, communities, and a strong core of volunteers. The support was priceless.

We were grateful for our partnerships with radio stations, news stations, the newspaper, restaurants, hair salons, barbershops, biker clubs, high schools, people in business, other churches, and civic representatives.

Through our many connections, we served many. We learned that partnering helped us to achieve greater results for God and uplifts His kingdom right where people need Him most, in their hearts.

Questions to Consider

What partnerships have influenced your impact in the community?

Who are your current partners? How do these relationships help support your vision?

What is the greatest asset you bring to the table? Does it benefit everyone at the table?

Imagine that you have unlimited resources and volunteer support? What can you imagine for your next project? How could you change your city? How could you impact the heart of the forgotten?

I AM EVANGELISM

CHAPTER 8
You Are Evangelism

"Honor is born from humility, not hierarchy."
–Deanna Hudgens

An evangelist is a servant of God, a voice for the Lord, and a witness for Jesus Christ.

An evangelist preaches the Gospel of the Kingdom of Heaven and introduces Jesus Christ as the door to enter into a life with God in His Kingdom.

Evangelists are big on showing honor to everyone, everywhere. They are committed to sharing Christ, no matter what.

I recall a situation that transpired during one of our evangelism events.

A gentleman began to harass the team. One of the team members called me over to speak with him. Somewhat in a hurry to get home to attend a wedding that afternoon, I remember thinking, *this man has been drinking, and he is*

I AM EVANGELISM

angry!

I had no clue what to say.

I walked over to the man and said the first thing that came to mind, "God loves you!"

The man looked at me intently. Five minutes later, he accepted Jesus Christ as his Lord and Savior!

When you do not know what else to say to a person, say, "*Jesus loves you.*" sincerely from your heart.

You can say Jesus loves you with confidence when you know the Father's love and what He's done for you.

You are evangelism because you know the redeeming power of your story. Be willing to tell any and everyone how God saved your soul.

You can share what He delivered you from and how long you have followed and served Him.

When I became born again, I didn't even know where the book of Genesis was, but I knew I was saved, free, clean, delivered, and at peace with God and myself.

If I could experience those feelings and that assurance, I know two things: 1) God is real, and 2) others need to know Him.

The first time I witnessed to someone, I had only been saved for two weeks.

At that time, I had only been drug-free for two weeks, but

God gave me grace every day. I wanted to share my testimony with everyone.

Days became weeks, weeks became months, months became years, and at some point, I had come too far to turn back.

Being drug-free became a lifestyle for me, and today, I am totally free. So, when I look into the eyes of an addict and say, "You're going to make it," I know what I'm talking about!

When I tell people, who have experienced a terrible divorce, "You will smile again," I know because I have lived through it.

When I say, "God's going to turn your situation around," I believe it with everything in me.

When we share our testimony with others, our story resonates, and Hope springs up. The shift begins.

While evangelism efforts are wonderful, preparation is critical. Sharing our story is vital and creates connection and relationship, but we also want to understand how to evangelize effectively.

Although our story and evangelism efforts are imperative, be mindful that our efforts are about winning souls and making disciples and not church growth.

The first church that I had an active role in ministry expansion was only about six months old.

God gave us wisdom to increase from 75 members to about 300 members in a few short months.

I AM EVANGELISM

It was apparent that the hand of God was upon this ministry.

The ministry was reaching young people, evangelizing, operating in gifts, living out prophetic words, being delivered, and, most of all, souls were being saved, and disciples were being raised!

In the growth process, be diligent about growing people, not numbers, creating life opportunities, not fads, winning souls not filling chairs.

Growing people, creating life opportunities, and winning souls, serve God. Seeking numbers, the latest fad, and filling chairs serves man.

Be mindful of remaining God-focused and committed to growing disciples rather than growing other things.

It does not take long for people to realize they are no longer the priority and have taken a back seat to pompous church growth.

One of my favorite quotes is, "People don't care how much you know until they know how much you care."

Evangelize with a pure heart.

Evangelize to honor God.

YOU ARE EVANGELISM

Questions to Consider

Do you remember the first time God used you to rescue a life?

How did that experience influence ministry for you personally?

What does it mean to you to give honor?

What is the usual effect of giving honor to another?

What are your top three ways to seek to keep your heart pure as God directs your steps?

I AM EVANGELISM

CHAPTER 9

Team Training

"I press toward the goal for the prize of the upward call of God in Christ Jesus." –Philippians 3:14

God blessed me with the mind of a playmaker. Even as a child, I did not want to sit on the bench the entire game, or at all in some cases. I wanted grass stains on my clothes, dirt under my nails, and sweat on my brow—the evidence of being involved and getting in the game.

I could not do any of those things sitting on the bench. For years, it bothered me that I had to sit on the sidelines and cheer for others.

I can recall times I chose not to pass the ball, and my coach pulled me out of the game because it showed a deficiency as a team player.

Looking back, I believe those moments were preparation for my work now because learning to sit on the bench and cheer for my teammates taught me the value and importance of teamwork.

Today, I prefer the team concept as I see the value and impact each member brings. We each bring something unique to the table, and when there is synergy, our differences come together to make us much more powerful and effective than when we are alone.

While I am committed to team ministry, I believe the training and support provided for leaders is vital.

As pastors and leaders, it is imperative that we, too, spend adequate time learning and growing in our call.

Likewise, it is equally important that we design systems that unearth gifts and encourage development in leaders and members because we do not evangelize alone.

The systems we employ are to enable individuals to discover and develop their strengths and gifts so that they can be deployed in their areas of expertise.

Similarly, when those with whom we serve see us learning and growing, they will be encouraged to do the same.

A leader that can grow with the team is a rare asset. It takes nothing away from them as a leader; rather, it enhances their ability to relate and remain adaptable while maintaining rock solid stability.

Pastoral Training

King David, son of Jesse, was responsible for taking care of the family livestock. He was the shepherd of the sheepfold. David took his role seriously. He understood accountability for his actions and his responsibilities as a leader. The weight of taking care of the sheep was no light or easy task.

If he lost one sheep, he knew it would directly impact his family.

He told Saul when a lion or bear came and took one of the lambs out of the flock, he went after it, struck it, and delivered the lamb from its mouth (1 Samuel 17:34-35).

He valued the life of each lamb.

However, with all of David's might, Jesse did not know he was raising a king.

Protecting the sheep from the bears and lions was God's way of training him to one day protect a nation.

David went to the next level when he defeated Goliath.

In all of his victories, David acknowledged God and his family and honored them with his life.

The same is true with becoming a minister of the Gospel.

As pastors, we honor God with our lives of service to Him, our family, then, ministry.

According to Ephesians 4:11-13, "Christ Himself gave the apostles, the prophets, the evangelists, the pastors, and the teachers to equip His people for works of service, so that the body of Christ may be built up until we all reach unity in the faith and in the knowledge of the Son of God and become mature, attaining to the whole measure of the fullness of Christ."

I AM EVANGELISM

Whomever God calls, He trains and equips to serve well and in one accord.

Years before becoming a pastor, I worked at two warehouses for eighteen years.

I drove forklifts, pulled orders, picked up heavy boxes, loaded and unloaded trucks, and data entry.

I had to commit to productivity every day, and I could not afford to make mistakes. Too many errors, abusing breaks, or arriving late would result in termination.

While the work was tedious, I had to remain focused.

God spoke to me one day and shared that everything I was learning was preparation for ministry.

I have found His words to be very true, of course!

Working in the warehouse, at the time, was equivalent to attending Bible School. I learned to work and remain committed, even when times were tough.

In the New Testament, the words pastor and shepherd are synonymous, indicating one who leads and stewards flocks.

Jeremiah 3:15 states, "I will give you pastors, which shall feed you with knowledge and understanding."

As pastors, when we accept the call, we must also accept the inherent responsibility and accountability to guide, protect, and feed the sheep, just as David did.

It is wise to identify moments of training in your life.

TEAM TRAINING

As you reflect on the journeys that prepared you to become a pastor and embrace the times you have learned how to lead, guide, protect, and serve God. Then, determine what you need to pass along in training and develop other leaders to do the same.

If you find there are areas in which you feel unprepared, seek training to sharpen your tools, and broaden your knowledge base.

Evangelism requires training. We must be willing to walk with and mentor individuals who desire a more meaningful walk with the Lord.

Leading by Example

Over the years, God taught me many things that made me more effective as a leader.

One of the first lessons I learned was leading by example. I quickly learned how important it is to model through leading. To do this effectively, preparation is of utmost importance.

At first, I was a "go with the flow" kind of minister, and my methods worked for a season.

Saturday after Saturday, roughly 100 people accepted Christ as their personal Savior. I remember thinking, *Look at God!*

However, the downside of that leadership style floated to the surface when the team got tired of spending countless hours preparing lessons, only to have me disregard their investment.

In the moment, I believed that God was leading me to do something else, and I wanted to respect the Lord's leading.

However, I learned that I should have adequately prepared to hear God while working as a team in the beginning stages of ministry.

At the time, I held weekly team meetings where decisions were made concerning conduct, behavior, and the order of events.

We spent hours planning and preparing to receive and serve the individuals who attended.

Having the heart of a shepherd, I wanted mercy for the child or parent who violated our rules during an event, although the team and I had agreed on different terms.

My actions frustrated our team's purpose and caused us to work overtime.

I learned that dynamic teams must honor each gift and personality at the table. At the same time, we must seek to understand one another and how each person operates to become the best version of ourselves, which creates the best version of the team.

Having systems in place to learn the heart of team members is wise. Working to develop relationships will serve you and the team well, both short and long-term.

Using personality inventories, team building exercises, and creating meaningful experiences will benefit the health and well-being of the team, and ultimately, the communities you serve.

TEAM TRAINING

Taking the time to look within and explore yourself, your motives, your actions will give the team permission to do the same. This type of introspective practice is healthy and will help to maintain humility, especially as God rewards the work.

Similarly, spending time with the team helps to understand what matters to them. It will enhance communication as well.

If you only train people to preach, they are not gaining all of the valuable tools needed to become effective leaders.

Preaching, as a stand-alone ability, does not equal leadership.

Fellowship

Once you have gathered basic information for all team members, it is critical to spend time getting to know them. What drives them? What inspires them? How do they interact with family and friends? How do they process information?

Fellowship is a natural way to spend time with team members and learn more about who they are and matters that are significant to them.

Team fellowship outside of the church walls as a group is a great way to get to know one another and establish relationships. It will significantly assist with the assignments the Lord gives as well.

Spending time with team members helps establish deeper connections and greater bonds—helping team members embody the spirit, voice, and vision of the ministry.

I AM EVANGELISM

I remember spending time together as a team after outreach efforts.

We would enjoy a meal together and talk about everything but outreach. We spent time talking about our children, exchanging jokes, and becoming closer by getting to know one another over pizza and wings.

Sometimes, we went back into the city and evangelized again.

Fellowship should be intentional and a form of service. Plan to spend time together. It will yield a high return.

Rules and Procedures

Another important aspect of training includes having rules and procedures. However, this is most effective after a relationship has been established among the team.

Rules and procedures are necessary for those serving and those being served because everyone sees life through their lens. It also helps to keep the team on the same page.

I recall several rules and procedures we had in place. A few included:

Rule #1: Bus drivers must have a Commercial Driver's License (CDL) endorsement on his or her license to operate a vehicle weighing 26,000 pounds or more. If people are transported, the licensee must have a passenger endorsement from the Department of Motor Vehicles (DMV).

Rule #2: A team member is required to assist bus drivers to help maintain order.

TEAM TRAINING

Rule #3: Only children 16 years old and older were allowed to ride the bus without the accompaniment of a parent or guardian.

Rule #4: Never give a child a ride alone, as you want to eliminate any potential risks. Remember, Satan is the accuser of the believer. Do not give him any fuel to start a fire.

Rule #5: When visiting a home, one cannot visit alone. Everyone must travel in groups of two or more.

Rule #6: Collect and gather names and addresses for giveaways, home visitations, and invitations to worship together.

Rule #7: Never witness to children from inside the car. Get out of the vehicle so that you can be identified.

Rule #8: Design and maintain rules for students.

Some rules for students included:

1. Everyone sits in a chair during the sermon to have his or her name entered into the giveaway to receive a prize.

Often during street ministry, many residents would watch and listen from a distance. To get them closer to the stage, we gave away prizes.

2. No gang colors or gang signs.

When ministering in multiple communities, you will learn about the influences of gangs. Therefore, it is essential to establish a standard early.

I AM EVANGELISM

I can recall at least 50 procedures we established for different situations. Many of them depended on the age group or setting (indoor or outdoor event, jail, prison, hospital, or school).

With years of street ministry, there were always new safety procedures put in place to protect parties on both sides.

Rules and guidelines are established to make the ministry function safely and productively. I would also recommend using common sense in situations that allow for individual discretion.

With your team, generate a list of rules and procedures that works for you to sustain ministry most effectively.

Training occurs in many different forms. However, training specifically for soul winning is key if you want to reach the lost!

Training establishes processes and protocols and creates an expectation for direction and outcomes.

If the goal is to see souls saved and people surrender their lives to Christ, creating opportunities for ongoing training to keep team members relevant and prepared is critical.

When thinking about evangelism, consider what the ministry will actively need.

Consider what type of training efforts will be necessary to engage in to start well and progress to the next level.

Being intentional about mentorship, attending conferences and workshops, and encouraging individuals to share how

TEAM TRAINING

God saved their lives will help grow the knowledge base of the leaders, build capacity, and support the desired evangelistic efforts.

Each team member should have a firm understanding of what Jesus has done for them, individually.

It is called their testimony – their story.

A heartfelt testimony is an amazing tool when engaging in evangelistic rescue missions.

Our testimonies give hope and hope does not disappoint.

Questions to Consider

Rules without relationship create short-term connections and even rebellion. What can you do to ensure relationships are valued beyond rules and regulations?

There are many ways to create fellowship opportunities without spending money. Can you think of three that could help any team with building relationships?

Training is a major investment. What type of training will best serve the needs of the ministry where you serve?

CHAPTER 10
Remaining Teachable

"No one reaches their destination alone."
–Hasker Hudgens, Jr.

Outside of my home, Mr. Johnson was my first mentor. He stopped by my house every Saturday morning to pick me up and take me to his home for work. Together, in the comfort of his backyard, we would chop wood, cut grass, and do other odds and ends around the property.

Mr. Johnson always had a story or something to share with me. We'd spend hours together, working, and talking. At the end of our time, he'd give me $10.00 for helping him. For a young Hasker, this was a nice payday, but the greater value was his investment in me. He was my introduction to mentorship. For this, I am forever grateful.

I learned so much from him, but I didn't realize the depth of the lessons he shared until I reached adulthood.

Mentorship is a major key to success in life and ministry.

I AM EVANGELISM

It will help you to avoid the potholes along the journey.

A good mentor will share lessons learned in life and provide information to advance and encourage you.

Leaders must be willing to walk with and mentor individuals who desire salvation or any significant changes in life.

Having resources and systems are necessary when evangelizing. However, mentorship and guidance are critical components of our development as leaders.

I like to say that training allow us to practice and learn from others before any misunderstandings or negative consequences. It can be a game changer in our efforts.

Exponential growth is possible with a well thought out training system.

While evangelists sometimes serve as mentors, it is equally important that they also experience mentorship.

From my mentors, I learned to create systems that yielded lasting results.

God shared wisdom through Pastor Jeff Allaway, Pastor Matthew Barnett, Pastor Randy White, Pastor Eric Redmond, the late Dr. Myles Munroe, Pastor Tony Miller, Pastor Ron Carpenter, and Pastor Bill Wilson (whom I mentioned earlier), to teach me lessons I still treasure today. I am forever changed for the better because of these relationships.

Pastor Jeff Allaway was the Director of Outreach at Phoenix First Assembly in Arizona (now Dream City Church) with Pastor Tommy Barnett. Pastor Jeff was in charge of scheduling and managing approximately 60 buses weekly. He taught me the importance of having systems that produce the desired results.

From Pastor Matthew Barnett of the LA Dream Center in Los Angeles, California, I learned firsthand, the power of picking up trash as a way to display care and love for the community.

I believe the Los Angeles Dream Center is one of the greatest models for outreach in the world. Their service is to the general population as well as the hurting. They have a leadership school, fitness center, disaster relief service, and more. Each month, they feed approximately 40,000 people.

From mainstream services to reaching the homeless, to ministering to those yet to discover their greatness, the Los Angeles Dream Center finds and heals the hurting places to reveal the hidden treasures within, waiting to be discovered.

I also learned a great deal from Pastor Randy White, the pastor of Without Walls Church in Tampa, Florida.

The name of the church alone suggests everything about its mission. From him, I learned to remain deliberate in the commitment to evangelize.

Without Walls Church held tent services, egg hunts, and formed community development corporations that afforded many people another chance at life.

Helping people become successful in the workplace or helping them obtain their General Education Development (GED) certificate, Without Walls Church is invested in supporting members of the community.

I AM EVANGELISM

Pastor Eric Redmond is roughly three years older than me, but many years wiser in the spirit. He was the person God used to teach, instruct, and counsel me. When we met, I had only been a believer for a few months.

Our encounter helped me establish a firm foundation in my walk with the Lord.

I traveled with him, drove him from place to place, carried his bible, and poured oil on his hands.

He licensed me to preach the Gospel and opened the door for me to begin to minister the Word of God!

In 1989, when I met the late Dr. Myles Munroe, he preached a message entitled, "Potential."

That message challenged me more than anything. The way I evaluated myself changed forever.

Dr. Myles asked five critical questions during that message.

He encouraged us to ask ourselves: *Who am I? Where am I from? Why am I here? What can I do? Where am I going?*

Those five questions sent me on a journey to discover my God-ordained purpose for life and ministry.

Consequently, the answers to those very questions were part of the reason I have spent decades winning souls and introducing as many people as I could to my Lord and Savior, Jesus Christ.

Revealing questions such as these help to identify purpose.

REMAINING TEACHABLE

Sadly, many people live life without any sense of purpose at all.

However, we were all birthed with purpose, and each of us is important to humanity.

Dr. Myles always made me feel important. A hundred people could have been waiting in line to have a short conversation with him. The crowd did not distract him from fully focusing on each person at hand. His attention honored the investment each person made by waiting.

The levels of interaction and attention Dr. Myles displayed with each person are important factors in ministry. You may see hundreds of people each week but, each week, those to whom you minister, only see one, you. Show them that they matter to you because they do. You may impart something extraordinary into their lives as Dr. Munroe did for me.

Bishop Tony Miller is the pastor of The Gate Church in Oklahoma City, Oklahoma (OKC).

For years, he was one of the most excellent examples of a mentor that I met with on a regular basis.

We met for breakfast every three or four months. When we finished eating, he would ask me what seemed like tough questions at the time. The questions were hard because I hadn't given them much thought.

Similar to Dr. Myles, he asked things like: *What is your vision? Where do you see yourself five years from now? How is your relationship with your wife and children? How's your devotional life?*

I AM EVANGELISM

His questions challenged me also. The Word tells us that without a vision, the people perish. However, a vision kept inside robs humanity of your divine influence. It must not be a secret.

Bishop Tony even invited me into his home to allow me to see him interacting with his family.

He also invited me, along with others, to annual retreats in the mountains. Modeling is powerful, and he is a master at it.

I experienced my first Mission Trip out of the country to the Fiji Islands with him. He also gave me opportunities to speak at his school, Destiny Bible College as well as the church he pastored. Bishop Tony Miller is a real deal mentor.

Pastor Ron Carpenter had the greatest ministry impact on my life. I could write pages, if not a book, on how God used him to groom, train, teach, and expose me to life in ministry.

He gave and demonstrated without end. He was a type of Elijah to me, and I took every opportunity to be Elisha. I kept my eyes on him.

I will forever be grateful for the apostolic anointing he imparted in me. It is a living gift.

Pastor Bill taught me more about ministry and life than anyone else, unabridged and uncut.

His clear and unapologetic approach to ministry was eye-opening and irreplaceable.

When I began learning from him through the Bus Ministry and Sidewalk Sunday School, Metro World Child reached close to 30,000 children and families weekly. Today, the ministry reaches close to 200,000 children each week.

The main idea of Metro World Child is, "the need is the call." If you can see and identify a need, you have been called to address that need. Looking the other way is simply not a part of their DNA.

Each week, we all pass the church (the people), on the way to the church (the building). If only we would look and identify the need and recognize the call, our world would change before our very eyes.

Time has proven Bill Wilson to be more than a mentor. I am honored to call him a brother and a friend.

I remember a time in my life when I was severely knocked down. Most of my associates walked away from me, but not Bill Wilson!

He got on a plane and flew 800 miles to Greenville, SC to look me square in my eyes to see for himself if I was okay.

We had breakfast. I drove him to the airport; he flew back to New York. Just like that, he demonstrated the sacrificial generosity of a true, covenant friendship. It still impacts my heart today.

What I learned from each of those men was extraordinarily life-changing.

The privilege of gaining such hands-on knowledge from each of these mentors was overwhelming.

Greenville, South Carolina would never be the same as God

showed us how to package the information from larger cities and fit it into the landscape of our community.

These were vital mentoring relationships that developed my leadership IQ and saved me time, energy, and errors.

As you work with mentors, the knowledge gained will not only enhance efforts to reach others, but it will also demonstrate the invaluable power of relationship and the impact it can have on others.

God has graciously given me several mentors who have helped me get to where I am in ministry and life.

1 Corinthians 4:15 states, "You have many instructors (tutors or mentors) but few fathers."

Two of the mentors I have been blessed with have given me stellar fatherly wisdom and care.

The areas in which a mentor can be beneficial are numerous. Their assignments could help with understanding the Word, finances, your health, and even developing discipline for life.

In some cases, I watched mentors on television each week for a few years. Those are individuals I call mentors from afar. I did not meet them, but I grew through their teaching and programs.

Others, I traveled to see when they were speaking within 200 miles of where I lived. They often kept me informed of their schedules.

In transparency, I was not always agreeable to associate on more than a ministry level. Unfortunately, some of the gifts

REMAINING TEACHABLE

we see in others and are attracted to, are accompanied with tough personalities.

Overall, mentorship is an opportunity to have a close, learning relationship with individuals with whom you share an interest.

It could be one who imparts into your life through speaking and teaching life lessons or someone whose books you read and apply towards your personal growth.

It could even be someone you listen to on the radio, television, or stream over the internet.

A mentor is someone you pursue that lights your fire.

Ultimately, a mentor is someone who puts his or her life down for another, a mentor-friend—willing to give freely, what they have worked years to obtain.

Questions to Consider

Do you have a mentor(s)?

In which area(s) do you still need mentorship?

How do you define and view mentorship?

Who are you mentoring?

Will you take a moment and write a Thank You note expressing your gratitude for your mentor(s)?

Will you take a moment and thank God for mentorship in your life?

CHAPTER 11

Volunteers and Vision

"Suppose one of you wants to build a tower. Won't you first sit down and estimate the cost to see if you have enough money to complete it?" –Luke 14:28

Volunteers are the heartbeat of outreach efforts. Without volunteers, reaching the masses becomes difficult.

The goal of my initial meeting with each volunteer was, and still is, to get acquainted.

We spend time getting to know each other through intentional communication.

First, I ask volunteers questions that tell me about themselves.

"What's your story or personal testimony? What has God put in your heart to do?"

"How can I help you accomplish this vision?"

Then I share my ministry story, how I became involved in

evangelism, and I communicate my passion for souls.

Then, I suggest that we help one another reach our goals together.

I say, "You help me with the mission at hand, and when your time comes to do what is in your heart, I will help you!"

For example, if a person desires to pastor a church, or pursue missions abroad, I make it a point to hold their dream in my head and heart. I remain intentional about reminding them of their vision every chance I get.

Extensive training is made available for all volunteers.

A large portion of that training consists of team building. Often, purpose is revealed during these times.

The key to being an effective servant leader in any organization is the ability to work as a positive, contributing member of the team while serving and trusting God to direct every mission.

One tool the Lord gave me to calm the anxieties of new volunteers was "Breaking Your Fears." This tool allows established leaders to intentionally take new volunteers by the hand and walk with them through a community and address their existing concerns or stereotypes.

Be aware that media outlets and the rumor mill can paint a picture that is quite different from reality.

To maintain the integrity of truth, we walk with them to provide a sense of security and to share ministry knowledge, as a group, while being outside of the traditional setting of the church.

As the new volunteers become more acquainted with each area, fears diminish, and they begin to identify how to best minister within each area.

It cannot be emphasized enough that there is safety in numbers. Highlight the importance of new volunteers not becoming overly confident. Lone rangers and self-appointed captains are extremely detrimental to the safety of the team and your reputation.

Create and teach the "Do's and Don'ts" of street ministry.

For example, when visiting a prison, never ask an inmate the reason they are serving a sentence, or how long they will remain incarcerated. As trust is developed, they will decide when or if they will share this information.

While evangelizing, it is wise to caution against general photography depending on the situation (which I know could be tricky in today's culture where everything is photographed and shared).

However, if photos are taken, it is mandatory for volunteers to gain permission from each person before taking their photo.

Consent forms secure approval should the volunteer plan to post any of the photos on social media sites, or on a web page.

All involved parties need to give written and verbal consent to avoid any potential liabilities.

I AM EVANGELISM

The do's and don'ts will adjust as ministry opportunities grow. Be observant and attentive.

Another key instruction God taught me is called Shadowing. It involves the careful selection and pairing of a tenured leader with a new volunteer during their first month.

If volunteers do not feel connected to the mission, vision, or others, their involvement can seem insignificant and cause them to step back.

If you place them alone right away, it could produce a false negative, and a stellar volunteer could slip through the cracks due to poor discernment and a lack of awareness.

Even with training and proper selection, they still may not have a complete understanding of how to effectively operate in their assignment. Keep them encouraged as they navigate new waters and territories.

Allow patience to have her perfect work as new volunteers make novice mistakes.

Whenever possible, create opportunities for volunteers to shadow a leader. The leader can properly equip volunteers to win souls while modeling the genuine heart of a servant.

As it pertains to ministry, I firmly believe the hand of one is the hand of all. We all win together, and we all grow together. There is no losing in serving God.

As a team, no person or ministry can function effectively as an island.

Establish early that the team is not in competition with one

VOLUNTEERS AND VISION

another in ministry.

Laying the groundwork for how the team will function is critical to the overall success of the training sessions.

Remind volunteers that everyone plays an integral part in the decision-making process.

Reinforce with volunteers that they are leaders, and their voice and experiences are vital in moving the vision forward.

Plan pep rallies! Motivate and inspire the team to continue *pressing toward the mark.*

I like to share specific heart-gripping testimonies of individuals to increase the faith and aptitude of the team. It is important not to grow weary in our well doing, and these accounts help to highlight what could have happened if no volunteers were serving God in the community.

We often ask ourselves challenging questions.

If not us, then who?

If not now, then when?

We needed to remain mindful of our why!

God is our why and serving Him requires commitment.

God is consistent, and we must be consistent as well.

Commitment from each volunteer is extremely beneficial for dependability in the planning process.

I AM EVANGELISM

Staff leaders help with the planning and logistics of each ministry event. Planning requires vision and management of resources, especially people.

Therefore, at the onset of each evangelistic assignment, staff leaders met with each volunteer for understanding and commitment to the vision and to sign a minimum one-year agreement.

Admittedly, it was not a foolproof approach. Some volunteers had work conflicts, while others simply did not keep their commitment. However, overall, it had more benefits than not.

We took the time to recruit individuals who had a hunger inside, a thirst to reach the broken-hearted, and compassion for the lost.

We started to recruit people with an appetite for the Father's heart.

Taking the Gospel of the Kingdom of Heaven to the streets is important work and deserves our most sincere commitment.

Many times, how people see you is how they will see your God. Therefore, team systems are critical to maintaining peace and order.

We established a highly effective team by assigning volunteers immediately upon receiving their commitment.

The process is slower, but retention increases.

Eventually, we were able to identify and retain the dedicated volunteers God sent for much longer, and these were people who were excited to fulfill the mission!

The key to getting people connected and committed is inspiring the shift from sitting in rows (going to church) to sitting in groups (being involved and connected)!

Groups are more effective than rows. It is difficult to commit to something in which you have no compassion or connection. Ministry needs compassion. People need connection. Sitting in groups facilitates both.

Leaders should remain available to answer questions and help guide volunteers along their journey as they discover who God created them to be, not who the leader wants them to be.

Evangelism is a dynamic ministry! It has many highs and lows, ins and outs, peaks and valleys.

When a person has the first thought about evangelizing, it can be defined in many ways because there are numerous ways to reach those that need God.

Practically, anything a person can do inside the four walls of the church can be adapted to the outside of the church. Singing, dancing, preaching, teaching, preparing meals, you name it—it's evangelism!

With so many opportunities, having volunteers is critical for smooth execution of evangelism efforts. Once their passion for serving God is identified, plug them in to serve!

I AM EVANGELISM

Questions to Consider

What creative ways can you serve God through evangelism?

Can you share your God-given vision in 60 seconds or less?

Have you developed patience for training volunteers? How can you help them to be successful in sharing God's heart?

How can you build connection within the ministry?

What is your system to activate volunteers?

CHAPTER 12

Soul Winning

"He who wins souls is wise." –Proverbs 11:30

Soul winning is becoming a bridge between the living and the dead in order to connect others to Jesus.

As leaders, everything we do can and should be done with soul winning in mind.

We can greet guests, receive tithes and offerings, and share announcements through the lens of presenting Jesus.

When we become intentional with our efforts, we will be amazed by the results.

People observe our actions all the time. They pay attention to our behaviors. Many are skeptical of witnessing love in operation. If we are not mindful of the details, we will miss opportunities to reach the lost.

Commit to winning souls in everything you do. When you decide to operate this way, everything has new meaning and purpose.

I AM EVANGELISM

Observing

Most Sundays, when the Word of God has gone forth, and a prayer of blessing is spoken over everyone for the upcoming week, I go to the front door to shake hands with everyone and hug the necks of babies and grandmothers.

As a pastor, it is important to remain available and accessible to your church family.

I love standing at the door until the last person has come through the line.

Throughout the years, I have noticed that most people appreciate that brief moment with their pastor. I know I did when I had it.

While some are in a hurry to go to work or get home for Sunday football, many people take the opportunity to introduce themselves and their families, say hello, or share an insight they gained from the message. Some even snap a few selfies!

Being available, touchable, and fully present creates an invaluable connection. It is also an opportunity to learn more about each life that comes through the door and share more about Jesus!

I have witnessed and learned a lot about people and human behaviors during the beginning stages of growing a ministry.

Some individuals see me at the door as a "seal the deal" moment before they get to the parking lot.

These individuals generally say, "I enjoyed myself, and I

will be back," *before* I can greet them. This always gets a chuckle out of me.

After hearing that line for the hundredth time, I realized these individuals might have felt that I wanted to hear this.

However, I have no other agenda than to greet each person and tell them what an honor it is to worship with them.

The goal is to make the experience as simple and impactful as possible for a person to come and leave without any pressure.

Allow newcomers (visitors) to choose a seat wherever they are comfortable.

It is not recommended to put the spotlight on them by asking them to stand and introduce themselves.

Paying attention to and respecting personal boundaries creates trust. Allowing people space to adjust represents Christ and His loving approach.

Over the years, I have observed that once a person visits for the third time, they are seriously considering establishing a new church home.

Still, we must be patient with their process. No one wants to be rushed into making this decision because joining a church is a big deal!

It is not like choosing a home or a new car. It is a major decision that impacts the trajectory of your walk with Christ through the voices that are allowed to shape your belief systems. It is a BIG deal!

I AM EVANGELISM

It is a serious commitment, and people need time to check things out and embrace their decision.

Also, because some people have been wounded by leadership elsewhere, they may want to know how the pastor and their spouse conduct themselves. What are they like? Are they friendly?

People often question, "Can I talk with them?" or "Will they judge me?"

Are there two or three people I have to navigate to get to them?

They want to know if the people in the church will receive them or if people will be suspicious of their motives.

Those with vision seek alignment with the vision of the house.

They consider their involvement at their last church and wonder where and if there will be room for them to grow with the ministry.

While most may not look to jump into ministry immediately, they are observing and asking questions like "Do I sense God's presence?"

For those who desire to teach or preach, it is important to have opportunities for them to grow in their gifts as they connect and serve.

Often, these opportunities naturally develop through weekly ministry needs, but faithfulness is non-negotiable for effective ministry and the growth of active ministers, both estab-

SOUL WINNING

lished and emerging.

People also visit churches hoping they will somehow stumble upon what they are called to do, as many have yet to discover the direction God desires for them.

A few are very clear about what they are called to and simply need guidance. While others blindly follow what someone told them they did well, never considering other areas.

Parents tend to observe the operation of the children's ministry and nursery. They want to know what their children will learn, who will teach them, and how decisions are made concerning them.

There are many considerations before a person knows if a church is for them and their family.

As a pastor, I understand the importance of great in-house ministries because growth is not limited to the sanctuary. It occurs not only when listening to sermons, but also when there is exposure to needs outside of our own.

First impressions are equally important.

Everyone from the parking lot volunteers to greeters, ushers, worship team, and more, are critical parts in setting an atmosphere where the Love of God can saturate and shift lives.

We must approach each area with soul winning in mind while putting our best foot forward.

At The Equipping Center (TEC), our motto is, "There are no bad days in Jesus!"

I AM EVANGELISM

Every day we wake up, it's a great day!

Whatever may have gone wrong before coming to serve God, we make sure it is not a hindrance to what needs to take place that day.

Sometimes it is helpful to find someone to agree with you in prayer so that you are not distracted and free to serve and worship.

The people whom the Lord will send to worship with you are not aware of what you may be dealing with on a personal level. They have no idea that life's challenges could be weighing you down. They are focused on being in church and having a meaningful worship experience.

As leaders, we understand that life happens to all of us, and sometimes we get to (not have to) minister while going through the storms of life remembering that God never abandons us and will show Himself strong as we stand strong in Him.

Training ourselves to stand strong in Him gives us the ability to minister to others who need to do the same. We need to be able to encourage those that were once on fire for Him but lost their zeal after being wounded in the church.

Some are often just one step from giving up on assembling together, and sadly, sometimes giving up on God. They need to know the answer is not to give up but to stand up!

Some have suffered or experienced "burnout" from other ministries and have placed a stake in the ground that they are not going to allow burnout to happen again.

SOUL WINNING

Burnout occurs when human effort is totally spent. Our spirits cannot experience burnout, only our flesh. Matthew 26:41 shows us that our spirit is always willing, but our flesh can become weak. We must minister through our spirit man, our inner man, and not through human effort.

Sometimes when burnout happens, people will look for a church where they can rest and refuel. They need to take things slow.

These individuals often attend and observe from the back.

Initially, they tend to be guarded, but as their inner man gets stronger, they move up a row or two and engage more.

Some people may be dealing with personal matters like a separation or divorce that has broken their spirit. Others could be grieving the death of a loved one, and they need a place to recover without interference; a place where they can soak in worship and allow the Word to heal them from the inside out.

There are also individuals who have gone back to familiar lifestyles they once gave up, and they are in search of God's restorative care. They too need a worship and recover without judgment and shame.

I have personally experienced many of these challenges in some way, and there is no doubt that God and worship were key to my survival and restoration.

Although anointed and called by God, during those times, people often "feel" like the complete opposite not wanting to do anything but hide.

They need to know that God has not changed His mind concerning them!

Being a person who has experienced ups and downs, peaks and valleys, great days and growth days (remember, there are no bad days in Jesus), I position myself to be a shepherd with a warm greeting, kind words, and gentle presence, understanding that God is always present to strengthen us in our weaknesses.

Because God first loved us, we are equipped to love others!

Some people are learning the saving Grace of God for the first time, while others are finding that He is still waiting for their return with open arms.

From an initial born-again experience to a prodigal returning home again, make it a point to understand there are many journeys present in a single service. There are so many people with a story to tell. It is important that we, not judge but, respect every story.

Making it a point to recognize where people are in their journey and what they need, helps them understand that you are concerned for them and leading them individually and intentionally.

When we quiet ourselves and lean into God's voice, our ability to see and discern is sharpened, and our desire to reach others grows.

Everything with Love

Another important concept in soul winning is showing love. To become an effective minister, you must genuinely care about people.

Never judge a person by their appearance, or listen to, or engage in negative reports about them from others. This is vital for authenticity and showing God's love to others.

It is our privilege to honor everyone and the fresh start God supplies.

The Word reminds us that He cleanses us all from sin and gives us new mercies every day. Daily He loads us with benefits, and forgiveness is one of them!

If God, who is without sin, can pour His love upon us, who are we to become judge and withhold love from others?

Everyone has a past! We have all done things we are not proud to confess. Yet, God loves us and wants us to walk in the newness of life.

This is why we cannot forget that while we were still sinners, God died for us and rescued us.

With this in mind, we must make a place for others to be found and restored by the unconditional and ever-forgetful love of God.

Outreach is a great place to start!

It is affordable and a direct way to value and reach the individual. When we show people their worth, it gives people hope—hope that does not disappoint. When lives are affirmed with value, this affirmation intimately and intentionally displays love for them and their journey to greatness in Christ!

I AM EVANGELISM

The foundation of our faith is love. Therefore, soul winning is a fundamental act of love.

It is far more than having the largest congregation.

If the motivation is to have large crowds, this can be accomplished without saving a single soul.

However, if the focus is to make a difference by reaching outside the walls of the church, and seeking the lost that they may be transformed, then, growth is inevitable.

It has been my personal experience that when evangelizing and building relationships in the community, you discover people have different needs because life is the cumulative effect of our individual experiences.

Evangelism requires time, energy, resources—and compassion, all while loving humanity.

It is rewarding, too!

However, the reward for your labor most likely will not come from the addict, the homeless, or the troubled teen.

It will likely not come from the hurting people you led to Jesus, but it will surely come. It is rewarding in itself to see lives turned around for God.

The big reward is knowing that doing the Will of God from the heart and winning souls pleases the Father. Proverbs 19:17 reads, "He who has pity on the poor lends to the Lord, and He will pay back what he has given."

Further, we have the promise, according to Ephesians 6:6-8,

SOUL WINNING

that what we make happen for others, God will make happen for us!

We have witnessed the reward of the Lord in more ways than can be counted. Doors opened for us that I could never have imagined nor opened by human effort. God did it!

I believe it is, in part, because we helped the hurting and the poor in their time of need, and when we were in need, God supplied.

A few of my favorite scriptures come from 1 Corinthians 3:5-12.

When witnessing to the lost, no matter what their social or economic status might be, your assignment is to sow seeds of love with love.

When sowing, trust God to send someone to water the seeds, as He is the one who gives the increase.

When we operate from a place of love, God will also send resources to help us reach even more souls.

Trust me when I say God will always be ahead of where you are!

Some people followed the bus or truck back to the church many times after a day of outreach, only to tell us they will join us the next day.

Others shared that they were looking for a church that was involved in the community.

We received countless monetary gifts anonymously from

people who saw the outreach team ministering in communities. They had passed us wearing those red t-shirts loving and serving others and wanted to support the work.

We received letters with checks with encouraging memo notes like *"Keep running those buses!" "I used to ride the bus!" and "to help you continue the work."*

No matter how much you do, there is simply no getting ahead of God!

When we show love genuinely and sincerely, God will shower us with blessings beyond our ability to count.

Loving and winning souls is essential to me because I was the child who needed a ride to church. I was the child who had fallen one grade behind in school and needed assistance with learning. I was the troubled teen who needed rescuing. I was the adult who had lost their way.

Having fancy church buildings, strategies to gain financial support, technological advances, and perfect atmospheres for families, are all wonderful initiatives, but our ultimate aim as believers is to "go into all the world and preach the gospel to every creature" (Mark 16:15).

Jesus said, "Upon this rock, I will build my church, and the gates of Hades shall not prevail against it" (Matthew 16:18).

God has equipped us with the keys to the kingdom of heaven, and whatever you bind on earth, will be bound in heaven, and whatever you loose on earth, will be loosed in heaven.

What a tremendous authority you've been given to win the lost and turn a nation back to our God!

SOUL WINNING

It has always been about people and the nations!

Beautiful buildings, big screens, lights, cameras, and smoke on the stage are appealing, but God didn't die for them. He died for you! He died for me!

If you want to populate heaven, love like our Father—you'll win more souls with love than anything else.

Remember the harvest truly is plentiful, but the laborers are few.

Labor from a place of love. Win more souls than you ever dreamed or imagined.

Pray to the Lord of the harvest...

I AM EVANGELISM

Questions to Consider

What is your experience with soul winning?

How has the Love of God changed your life?

How can you share this Love with others?

The Bible says that Love never fails. What does that say about Love being the focus for evangelism?

Can you see the harvest? Ask God to show you.

CHAPTER 13

A Passion for Souls

"Good will always be the enemy of great!" –Jim Collins

I can still hear their words, "You'll be back in two weeks!" Perhaps for the wrong reasons, but at that moment, I realized I needed to prove my friends wrong.

I also realized that as I told my friends about the changes taking place within me, I was burning bridges and tearing down strongholds that led to my old life.

In other words, I was not turning back. There was nothing back there but death.

I started my heavenly journey, and I was passionate about pursuing Jesus with my all.

That pursuit has placed me on a path I could not have designed. It has led me to God's most significant responsibility for me; going into all the world and preaching the Gospel.

I AM EVANGELISM

The Father uses everything for His glory. Although we do not always understand His process, we can trust His plan.

Every experience He leads us to builds us, and it adds to our ability to help others know Him.

Being made in His image and His likeness (Genesis 1:26), God has placed greatness inside everyone. He is passionate about it being shared with others.

Just as He told Abraham in Genesis 12:2, "I will make you a great nation; I will bless you and make your name great, and you shall be a blessing."

You are indeed a blessing, destined to make a difference in this world.

Pursue God with everything you are and encourage others to do the same.

Share what God has done in your life.

God sees the person He created, not the person you deem unworthy.

Remember, Peter denied Jesus, but God saw a rock.

Gideon was full of fear, but God called him a mighty man of valor.

Moses murdered a man and was on the run! God looked at him and saw a man called to deliver a nation out of slavery into freedom!

God sees greatness in you, too!

Jim Collins, in his book *Good to Great,* states, "Good will always be the enemy of great!"

How does anyone argue with that thought?

Settle it today! There is nothing average about you!

God sees extraordinary in you!

He sees victory! It is a victory that was yours before you were ever born.

He is not looking at the divorce you experienced, or the child support you could not pay.

He is not focused on yesterday. He is in your today.

I am a witness. You will win if you don't quit. Follow God with passion.

Follow Him with great energy, strength, and zeal. God will put you on top and sustain you!

He always positions His children to win!

Never fear the faces of men!

There is a world waiting to know Him, longing for validation, and acceptance.

Give them the gift you have been given.

They may act as though they don't need God but reach out still. Share Jesus Christ.

I AM EVANGELISM

Be passionate about their soul, knowing the value it has to our Father.

We are all commissioned to go and spread the good news of the Gospel wherever and whenever the opportunity arises.

When we accept Christ into our lives, the door is opened to greatness, and we can share that greatness door by door!

Over the years, I've had many functions. However, my favorites include *husband and father*.

Still, if you asked a thousand ministers and believers from Greenville, South Carolina to the continent of Africa to describe me, I believe without fail, the response would be Evangelist!

I am humbled by the life I live and what God has prepared for me. I have made a lot of mistakes, and as I confess my sins, I find He is faithful and just to forgive me, just as it is written. He said if we call upon Him, He will answer and show us great and mighty things. He has definitely kept His promises with me.

My life is living proof of what can happen when God wins your soul. I didn't find evangelism. Evangelism found me and led me on a path that has shaped the entire course of my born-again life. There's not a day that I don't think about some part of soul winning.

So, I guess it's true…I Am Evangelism!

Now, the question is…Who are you?

PRAYER

You made it! You finished the book.

Now, please allow me an opportunity to pray with you. We may never meet, although I hope we will.

As you have read my story, I pray that your story will take wings and fly.

God created you for such a time as this. No one has chosen his or her birthday, so we know the Father has given you life, equipped you for the journey, and now, here you are!

Get up, suit up, lace up, and face up!

Your future is waiting for you along with a crowd of people who have no clue what to do with their lives.

God has sent you to rescue them by His Spirit. So today, and each time you revisit this book, this prayer is for you and discovering what can happen when God wins your soul.

Thank you for getting this far.

PRAYER

Now, finish strong. Light a fire and run!

In the name of our Lord and Savior, Jesus, the Christ, Father, we thank you.

I stand with this highly prized, valued, and determined reader, to say thank you.

Thank You for the privilege of life with You and in You.

Life with You because You created us for such a time as this with ordered steps that we would walk in purpose with goodness and mercy following us all the days of our lives.

Life in You because it is in You that we live, and move, and have our very being.

We are lifeless without You, the Giver of Life.

As we remember the many paths that we have walked, some scary, some brightly lit, some dim, some lonely, no matter the road, we can look and see You, faithful and true.

You have always been there.

You sheltered us when we absolutely knew we would die, but here we are—alive to testify of Your faithfulness.

We can now say with understanding that we have tasted and seen that You are good.

To those who may have lost trust, may our survival stand as living proof that You are trustworthy.

To those who may have given up, may our endurance stand

PRAYER

as proof that You are our strength.

To those who may have been deceived, may our stories stand as proof that You are faithful and You are true.

To those who may have been abandoned, may our lives stand as proof that You are always with us.

Help us to continue to look within and discover the "me" You created us to be.

Father, help us to desire the work of the evangelist.

Help us to take courage and embrace every opportunity to introduce our Lord and Savior, Jesus Christ, to the lost souls that we meet each day.

May we not fear the faces of men or what they may think about our willingness to follow You.

I declare that we are doers of Your Word and not hearers (or readers) only.

It is established that we will carry out the Great Commission to go!

Today, we look up!

The Gospel of the Kingdom is at hand, and the Spirit of the Evangelist is released!

Every knee shall bow, and every tongue confess that Jesus Christ is Lord, to the glory of the Father!

Today, we shout, Yes! We will GO!

A Sinner's Prayer

Lord, I need you.

I know there is no living without you.

I confess with my mouth that Jesus Christ is Lord.

I believe in my heart that God raised Him from the dead.

Lord, I confess my sins to You and ask You to save me.

Thank You for not giving up on me.

Please teach me the purpose and meaning of my life.

Help me to follow and live for You.

In the name of Jesus, Amen.

From My Wife

I believe we all can agree that how we treat one another matters.

How we value or devalue the life of another person matters.

If we choose to seek potential rather than mistakes, matters.

It has been said that people don't care how much you know until they know how much you care.

Caring is a heart issue. Caring says your heart matters.

God has blessed me and countless others to engage in a relationship with a person who exemplifies all of the good things I have mentioned. That person is the author of this book, Mr. Hasker Hudgens, Jr.

He is, at his core, a remarkable man, and it is my great joy and honor to be his wife. His relationship with Jesus brings immense joy and privilege into my life.

I have rarely seen such a continual offering of the Grace of

FROM MY WIFE

God right before my very eyes.

Each morning, I awaken to Grace. Each night, I lie down with Grace. I guess I have a double portion of God's unmerited blessing and favor.

In Hasker's presence, everyone is welcomed, accepted, encouraged, celebrated, and heard, just as God did for him.

It is what I call his "Grace Gift."

The Lord says, "Freely you have received, freely give."

When Grace was distributed, I am sure that Hasker received a double portion as well.

Grace does for us what we cannot do for ourselves, while Love chooses to give us what we could never afford.

When these two virtues connect in a leader, you find yourself on the receiving end of an extraordinary relationship that allows the unconditional love and adoration of God to meet you with open arms.

It is God's way of cutting through all the red tape and disappointments of life, to get to you and celebrate you!

You survived and are surviving!

Sometimes people are so consumed with the disappointments that they fail to realize they survived!

Hasker Hudgens, Jr. has been anointed by God to help you focus and see that life's challenges (poverty, disqualification, minimal resources, and past records) are simply opportunities

FROM MY WIFE

to see what a loving God can do when He wins your soul.

Often, the Holy Spirit will move through someone to reach out and do for us what we cannot do for ourselves.

I have witnessed the Holy Spirit use Hasker Hudgens, Jr. to purge decades of guilt and shame simply by recognizing that there is still value after trauma, life after a broken heart.

I believe we all have experienced a broken heart in one way or another.

I have seen him, in a look, restore confidence (in God) and cause a despairing soul to trust God one... more... time.

I have watched his determination to mend broken relationships, to love those who have been overlooked, and to show what God can do as He knocks on the door of a heart to heal it.

Simply put, it is what God does and has done through him, heart-by-heart, generation-by-generation, soul-by-soul, door-by-door.

Right when you think the bottom is falling out, God sends a man with a net and a Word.

As a result, many find care and encouragement during both growth days as well as great days of celebration.

Oftentimes, when in a crowd, from the East Coast to the West, someone will shout out, "Pops!" or "Dad!" as we walk along.

They are beautiful reminders of blessings from God, far and

FROM MY WIFE

near, strategically placed along life's journey.

I am grateful to witness such life-changing joy, first-hand.

In closing, if you ever hit a rough patch in life where you seem to be all alone, I pray that God sends a mender for you, a mender like Hasker Hudgens, Jr.

With grace and love flowing, they will not allow you to give up on God's plan for you.

There is profit in all work. They will take you by the hand and remind you of all you still have to work with inside you.

Allow them to lead you back to the Father for a fresh start, just as Hasker Hudgens, Jr. has done for so many.

For him, *I Am Evangelism* is not just a book. It is his life's assignment as a soul winner.

I am humbled to love him, privileged to respect him, and forever grateful to answer the call with him.

Together…We Are Evangelism!

Deanna Hudgens, Wife

From My Daughter

People often ask me how I decided to become an addictions counselor.

Honestly, the answer is simple; I believe I was called to do this work.

Addictions Counseling chose me; I didn't choose it.

I was about three or four years old when my father accepted Jesus as his Lord and Savior, so I don't have any memory of him living in active addiction.

I don't know what it would be like for my parent to use drugs or alcohol in front of me, to abuse me, or put my life in harm's way to support a habit.

I don't know what it's like to go without because my parent spent all of his money supporting his habit, and I am blessed never to have had to visit my father behind bars.

I call my experience grace and mercy!

FROM MY DAUGHTER

My siblings and I are blessed never to have witnessed the things that children do from growing up with an addicted parent.

However, in my line of work, I have worked with children and parents who have suffered because of addiction.

On paper, I am a licensed professional counselor and master addictions counselor, but more importantly, I am a child of God who recognizes counseling as my ministry.

When I entered the field of counseling, I was sent to work with teenagers in Greenville, South Carolina, who were referred for counseling due to alcohol and drug use.

Somewhere along the way, the opportunity came to lead a group of adults who were struggling to get clean.

Back then, the most popular substance among teens was Marijuana, and among adults, substance abuse varied from person to person.

I often ran into people who attended church with either my father or my grandparents. They appeared embarrassed to see me and looked worried that I might judge them.

I even encountered some of the teens who attended Operation Go! and what I learned early on by watching my father operate in his gift is that people in those predicaments needed me to show them compassion.

I remember being frustrated with my job as the duties given to me continued to pile higher and higher.

One Wednesday night after service, I waited as my dad took

FROM MY DAUGHTER

the time to speak to members who were in a long line to talk to him or receive prayer.

He was the evangelist at Redemption World Outreach Center at the time, and the people who waited to talk to him stood in line almost every Sunday and Wednesday (They did this for years).

When I was younger, my siblings and I would become frustrated that he would take so much time with people after church, but eventually, I learned the reason why.

He was operating in his gift, and we were too immature to understand it at the time.

That Wednesday night, I shared with my father how frustrated I was with my position at work, and he shared a story with me about his former job at Granger.

He told me I needed to make my job my ministry.

I was frustrated with his answer, but I prayed about it that night, and God gave me clarity about the situation.

I'll never forget that day because it was a defining moment in my career.

Once I made my job my ministry, my outlook on everything changed, and I believe I became more impactful at work.

God used me during that time to prepare me for work that would require the same commitment, dedication, and tenacity that I learned years before while volunteering alongside my father and many others in Operation GO!

FROM MY DAUGHTER

In 2012, I was hired as a manager of a treatment program that treated court-ordered individuals.

I thought I was ready based on my experience, but what I saw was more hurt and pain caused by addiction than I had been accustomed to seeing.

This was six years after I began my work in Greenville, South Carolina, and now I was in the Metro Atlanta area of Georgia working with numerous clients who were fighting addictions involving harder, more complex substances such as Methamphetamine, Heroin, or prescription drugs. For the first time in my life, I had clients die from having an overdose.

I heard horrific stories of loss and family brokenness due to addiction.

Working in the program, I also witnessed people work for two years to complete the program and reunite with their children that they hadn't connected with in years.

I saw people work the 12-step program and reconnect with God like never before.

Many of them shared it was because of the grace of God that they were able to make it through.

While addiction is ugly, God can give you beauty for ashes, just as He did for my father over 30 years ago.

Saying yes to God and turning your back on your old ways will undoubtedly change the trajectory of your life and your family's life and put an end to generational curses.

FROM MY DAUGHTER

I am grateful for the lessons my father taught me as a little girl. He is evangelism, and because he encouraged me to make my job my ministry, I am evangelism, too!

Tamika Hudgens Grimes, Daughter

ENDORSEMENTS

This book is full of practical strategies to win souls for Christ. Pastor Hasker Hudgens, Jr. has given us the "How To" guide for evangelism and how to reach God's lost sheep. This book is a must have, must read, and must apply book and guide. Thank you, Pastor, for blessing the Body of Christ with the tools and resources to live out the heart of God through our daily witness of His grace and love toward us.

Sean Dogan
Senior Pastor, Long Branch Baptist Church
Greenville, SC

With the heart of a pastor and the courage of an evangelist, Pastor Hasker Hudgens, Jr. authentically shares his passion for souls. He offers to us his undeniable unwavering confidence that what God has promised is available to every person.

This book shows us how to ensure that each person we encounter is infused with the love and message of Christ. As you read, you will rejoice at the practical yet skillful way

ENDORSEMENTS

Pastor Hasker leads us to the streets to experience what only God can do- transform the hearts of men.

Whatever your call to ministry, be empowered by this excellent example of 2 Timothy 4:5 to do the work of an evangelist and fulfill the duties of ministry to the glory of God.

> Nicole Spain White
> Executive Pastor, Pure Dominion Ministries
> Elgin, SC

I have personally known Pastor Hasker Hudgens, Jr. for a decade and known of him for twenty plus years. He lives what he preaches! He not only knows the biblical truths of outreach, but he also knows how to implement them relevantly. Anything he has to say on any subject is worth listening to. He has earned the right!

> D. Chris Thompson
> President/Pastor, Holmes Bible College/Memorial Church
> Greenville, SC

In my over 30 years of ministry, I've probably never met anyone as skilled in street ministry as Pastor Hasker Hudgens. I've personally watched him move through different communities and people groups, understanding their needs, and taking the gospel to them with great success. If you want a real "rubber meets the road" evangelistic tool, I highly recommend this book.

> Pastor Ron Carpenter, Jr.
> Redemption World Outreach Center
> San Jose, CA

ENDORSEMENTS

"Pastor Hasker is an influencer to the influential. His approach to evangelism is transparent and authentic. He is the key lever in building and equipping a ministry to win souls effectively."

Alphaeus Anderson
Youth Magnet, Author
Greenville, SC

I know of no one better to speak on the subject of evangelism within an urban, African American context than Hasker Hudgens, Jr. His personal story and strategies have directly transformed thousands across the Upstate of South Carolina and indirectly impacted millions around the world.

He was mentored by the best to the extent that he has become one of the best voices on evangelism.

Although much of his work has been in the African American context, the principles and strategies given by the Holy Spirit are applicable anywhere. Whenever my wife and I are in Greenville, SC, having dinner with him and Deanna, we know people or their parents, who were saved through his outreach efforts, will stop him constantly.

He's indeed a spiritual father to the Upstate of South Carolina and an ambassador for evangelism worldwide.

Bishop Marcus Benjamin
The Benjamin Agency
Charlotte, NC

ABOUT THE AUTHOR

Hasker Hudgens, Jr. has a strong commitment and passion for activating the "leader within the leader."

Utilizing 20+ years of education and experience as a lecturer, teacher, consultant, leadership trainer, mentor, and pastor, he is faithful to deliver relevant and compelling, life-changing teachings that open perspectives and impact lives on generational levels.

ABOUT THE AUTHOR

His loyalty to and understanding of the importance of purpose has enabled him to consult and serve corporations, civic leaders, and countless organizations and ministries around the world.

As an accomplished international speaker, effective trainer, and inspirational motivator, Hasker has trained and conducted workshops throughout the United States and abroad in various regions of Africa, South America, Mexico, Haiti, and the Fiji Islands.

Hasker addresses churches, corporate entities, local charities, and civic organizations.

He serves on several philanthropic boards and business roundtables, adding balanced and comprehensive insights to solutions and plans of action.

His list of accolades includes various mayoral and senate proclamations and recognitions including the South Carolina Palmetto Patriot Award which is the highest honor bestowed by the Office of the Lieutenant Governor recognizing individuals who have made outstanding contributions to the citizenry of the State of South Carolina.

Having served in ministry since 1992, on February 9, 2014, a long-standing promise from God became a reality, and The Equipping Center was born as a community of believers in the Lord Jesus Christ with a passion for living the promises of God and their God-given purpose, where he is the Senior Pastor.

Hasker resides in Greenville, South Carolina and is happily married to Deanna Hudgens. Together, they are committed to loving God, loving family, and loving and equipping

ABOUT THE AUTHOR

individuals for the work of ministry.

To learn more, visit www.iamevangelism.com.

THE EQUIPPING CENTER

Armed with the charge of Ephesians 4, The Equipping Center (TEC) is committed to loving and equipping the saints for the work of ministry. TEC works to edify the body of Christ, until we all come to the unity of the faith, and the knowledge of the Son of God.

God established TEC to help individuals discover, develop, and deploy their gifts for service to Him. It is our life's work to interrupt the destructive effects of the world's systems and introduce the culture of the Kingdom of Heaven, restoring health to the Church and purpose to each individual.

Visit us on the web at www.theequippingcenter.co.